HUMMINGBIRDS:
MY WINTER GUESTS

Also by Arnette Heidcamp

Bluebirds in My House

Rosie: My Rufous Hummingbird

A Hummingbird in My House

HUMMINGBIRDS:
MY WINTER GUESTS

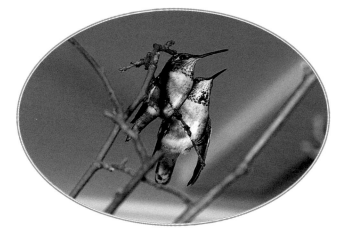

ARNETTE HEIDCAMP

WITH DRAWINGS AND PHOTOGRAPHS
BY THE AUTHOR

Crown Publishers, Inc.
New York

Published by Crown Publishers, Inc., 201 East 50th Street, New York, New York 10022.
Member of the Crown Publishing Group.
Random House, Inc. New York, Toronto, London, Sydney, Auckland
http://www.randomhouse.com/
CROWN is a trademark of Crown Publishers, Inc.

Printed in China

Design by Mercedes Everett
Spot illustrations by Jennifer Harper

Library of Congress Cataloging-in-Publication Data
Heidcamp, Arnette.
Hummingbirds : my winter guests / Arnette Heidcamp. — 1st ed.
p.   cm.
1. Hummingbirds as pets—New York (State)   2. Ruby-throated
hummingbird—New York (State)   3. Rufous hummingbird—New York
(State)   I. Title.
SF473.H84H453   1997
636.6—dc21   97-646
CIP
ISBN 0-517-70884-1
10   9   8   7   6   5   4   3   2   1
First Edition

There are many precious little hummingbirds
who get caught in life's snags.

This book is dedicated to them
and to those who help them.

*Nature really outdid herself when she
created these tiniest of treasures, the hummingbirds*

CONTENTS

HUMMINGBIRDS:
MY WINTER GUESTS

INTRODUCTION

On September 20, 1995, the telephone rang. It was police dispatcher Kate Scheffel. "Is this Hummingbirds 911?" I smiled. "Yes, I suppose it is," I responded, but Kate wasn't being funny. She sounded a bit distraught as she asked me to take in an injured hummingbird that she had found.

Time and again her question has come back to mind . . . *Hummingbirds 911* . . . and each time it would rouse memories of the many injured or displaced hummingbirds in need of rescue that had taken refuge in my sunroom, from Squeak right up to the four spending the 1995/96 winter with me, each bird with its own unique story. Some have shown a remarkable will to survive after harrowing experiences. And thus, the nucleus of an idea for another hummingbird book was born.

Just as with the *Rosie* book, I hadn't been planning another on hummingbirds. Oh, perhaps something as noteworthy as a return visit from one of my former guests —or the highly unlikely event of a new species—but Kate's question and having had several hummingbirds winter here together have changed my plans. Perhaps I shouldn't be so hasty in my thinking—hummingbirds are so full of surprises that a pair and the offspring they produce may grace my sunroom and be the genesis of a future hummingbird book.

Having more than one has added a new dimension to my hummingbird experiences, surpassing by far all that I had previously experienced. While it is easy to love and enjoy each bird that stays, having more than one is just plain fun—their antics, their behavior toward one another, their surprises. The story of their time here begs to be told.

And, too, there is an insatiable curiosity about these glittering little bundles of energy. So many people have expressed a desire for me to write more about my adventures with hummingbirds. They have enjoyed becoming acquainted with the individuals as much as I've enjoyed working on these projects. And for me, these are journals or diaries of my experiences, complete with pictures. When I go back and read the books—as I do—I live these wonderful experiences again through my memories, and my enjoyment of these birds is extended. I've gotten what I consider to be precious glimpses into the private life of my favorite birds, the hummingbirds. I've gotten to know some darling individuals on an intimate basis—experiences I wouldn't trade for anything. There are days when I consider myself the luckiest person in the world, and sharing these experiences with other hummingbird fans has opened up even more doors.

I've made so many new and wonderful friends, people

who have written to express their thoughts and share *their* interesting experiences. Hummingbird fans are the nicest people, sincere and so dedicated to their little feathered friends. While the response that I've gotten has been wonderful, I think the most gratifying aspect of my books—and one that I had never even considered—is that other people who find hummingbirds in need of help are less afraid to give it, whether that means contacting a rehabilitator, undertaking the elaborate measures that Geoff Dennis of Rhode Island did to winter over the state's first rufous hummingbird, or spending every waking hour Jim and Brian had to care for Rupert, a ruby-throated hummingbird. We do everything we can to attract these little gems, and when we do, we cater to their every whim to keep them coming back. Hummingbirds became quite popular a few years back, and I remember thinking, "What a wonderful fad." But I knew the truth; once we fall under the spell of the hummingbird, it is not a fad, it becomes a passion.

For most of my life, I must admit, I've hated winter. I don't like winter sports or being outside at all, for that matter. I don't like the cold. I guess I've always felt that the only good thing about winter is that it ends—eventually. But the most unlikely of all creatures—one practically synonymous with summer, the hummingbird—has finally, after all these years, given me something to look forward to during the dark side of the year.

I thought Squeak was a once-in-a-lifetime visit that just happened by chance. I was in the right place at the right time—or, rather, he was. Then, when Rosie arrived, I couldn't believe my eyes—it is a picture indelibly etched in my mind. I was astonished. Surely nothing like this could *ever* happen again, right? Wrong! It can, and it has. They seem to be so endlessly full of surprises.

Hummingbirds 911 . . . As each of their little faces drifts past my mind's eye, I think about how it all came about, and my imagination tells me that those little spirits of summer may pass along gossip and information to one another, as bees do. "If you're ever stuck in the Northeast, I know this great little bed and breakfast. . . ."

From Hummingbirds in My Garden to Hummingbirds in My House

Late May to early June is my favorite time of year—floral abundance; picture-perfect greenery, still with a hint of spring. The fragrance of lilac, viburnum, and mock orange fills the air. Birds, busy with nesting chores, greet each morning with their beautiful, cheery songs. And belligerent male hummingbirds establish and defend their territories. As our reward for January, June frequently gives us stellar days with superb weather; it is often perfect. Yet I remember one particular June 2—what now seems like ages ago—that wasn't quite so heavenly. It was my birthday and I was all alone, feeling a little sorry for myself. I probably didn't like my birthday gifts, or hadn't gotten them yet. I hadn't seen any hummingbirds—at least that day—and cleaning, changing, and hanging a feeder was beginning to look more and more like an exercise in futility. To add insult to injury, it was unseasonably cold, a rainy 45 degrees F., and I was using some precious vacation time to sit in misery. I guess nothing was going my way. Then, a female hummingbird appeared and visited the lilacs. When she finished, she flew to the feeder and took a sip. That drink was followed by one after another. And thus, with that little sip and after working so hard to attract them, my relationship with hummingbirds in my garden had begun.

Eventually, of course, other hummers followed and the numbers swelled—four, six, eight, many juveniles. I thrilled at seeing four young hummers using a feeder at one time. In some years, late in the season, there were as many as twenty-five or thirty, counting both adults and immatures. Essentially the rubythroat is a woodland bird, frequenting woodland and meadow edges, riparian areas, and other places rich in flowers and vegetation. Their numbers are greatest in such habitats, so for my area, which is a little more open, twenty-five is a staggering amount. In the beginning the only thing I knew about hummingbirds was that I liked them. For years I wasn't much different from anyone else: I admired and enjoyed them from a distance and was in absolute awe when they came closer. Nothing was planted in the garden unless the hummingbirds would use it. I added feeders to keep them close. I observed them constantly and learned to recognize identifiable individuals.

Before we put a screen on the door leading from the sunroom to the backyard, I'd make sure the ceiling fan was off and then just leave the door open for more fresh air. One day while I was working at one of the flower beds, my daughter informed me that a hummingbird had entered the sunroom and was flying around inside. Apparently one adult male had chased another right into the house. When I went inside, the bird flew past me to go back outside, but then another flew back into the sunroom from my kitchen! Since there is a short, not-too-bright hallway and a turn between the kitchen and sunroom, I had never considered turning that fan off, too. It was right after that incident that the screen went up.

Whenever I go out to the backyard from the sunroom, I open the door and first peer out to make sure there are no hummers at the feeder under the spruce tree a few feet from the door—I wouldn't want to startle them. One day I opened the screen door leading out, and as I opened it, two immature hummingbirds participating in one of their never-ending chases sailed past my head and entered the room, one in pursuit of the other. They flew around inside for a minute or so, and then over to the window and clung to a window screen. I picked them up, one in each hand, and brought them outside. I then opened my hands and

Squeak—he changed the course of my life forever

released them. Shiny, emerald-green-tipped feathers covering a three-gram body no larger than the tip of a thumb,
they were so small that I was a bit afraid to touch them.
Hold a dime in your hand and close your eyes—imagine a
hummingbird! Those birds were born in a nest in the
maple tree in front of my house, and after fledging were
around my yard almost all the time. They entered the sunroom so often that eventually I took a window screen
down and the sunroom became just another part of their
territory. In the door, out the window, over and over,
around and around. They never seemed to tire, and I
never tired of watching them. I enjoyed their antics by
the hour. I knew how empty the yard would seem without

their twitters, squeaks, squeals, and chatters come fall, and I wished they'd decide not to leave but to winter right here with me.

Because of these birds' willingness to enter the sunroom, I felt comfortable offering it at other critical times, such as during Hurricane Gloria or other particularly strong storms, as well as during an early October freak, wet snowstorm. The thought of an unprotected hummingbird being pelted by hail or life-size raindrops won my sympathy. And thus began the transition from hummingbirds in my garden to hummingbirds in my house.

Then, many years later, another hummingbird entered the picture and changed the course of my life forever. That hummingbird was Squeak.

The end of summer is different for each person. For some it occurs with the geese flying south, with Labor Day, or when the children return to school; for some it is the first frost, the first freeze, or the advent of colder weather in general. For me, summer slips away with the hummingbirds, and the last day of summer is the day the last hummer departs—usually by the first week of October. Summer had been finished for weeks according to my criteria, and I had resigned myself to the fact that I wouldn't see any hummingbirds for months—always such a sad time for me. Then, when I went outside to feed the birds one morning in late October 1988, I found Squeak, searching for nectar among frozen flowers. I had no idea that my life was on the brink of its biggest changes ever, nor any idea that a few short years later I would be devoting myself to these marvelous little creatures on a full-time basis.

I recall how apprehensive I had been about my chances with Squeak, as I have been with each new venture into uncharted hummingbird waters. Who would ever have imagined, almost twenty years ago when I was so thrilled by that first visitor, that I would have them buzzing around my head in my own house?

There hasn't been one day that has gone by in the last several years that I haven't seen a hummingbird—most of them intimately. This winter I've had more hummers than humans residing at my home; maybe I should consider enlarging their sunroom. But even now, as incredible as it may seem, the hummingbirds still amaze and surprise me.

Squeak was *the* hummingbird in my house. Eventually, of course, others followed and the hummer numbers swelled—two, four . . . sound familiar?

RESCUED RUBYTHROATS

I wasn't expecting it. I hadn't even thought about it, but I suppose it was inevitable. Once the *Squeak* book was released, I would be called regarding other sick, injured, stranded, or otherwise misguided hummers caught in life's snags. When called upon for help, I *had* to give it. Although you know that some may not make it, you do what you can for all of them. Those birds that recover and go on to become healthy are so rewarding.

Hummingbirds are intelligent, resourceful, and adaptable within their niche. Some are hardy and well adapted to a range of conditions. They may be found living or nesting over a wide variety of habitats, from mountains to valleys, forests to deserts. Some make almost unbelievable migrations. The rubythroat crosses the Gulf of Mexico, a journey made possible by the storage of an extra $2\frac{1}{2}$ to 3 grams of fat, the roughly $22\frac{1}{2}$ to 27 calories necessary to make such a trip. The rufous migrates more than two thousand miles from its wintering to nesting area and crosses mountains 12,000 to 14,000 feet high on its return to Mexico. Some birds nest under harsh or extreme conditions, such as Costa's hummingbird of our Southwestern deserts. But in many ways, hummingbirds are delicate, finely tuned little specialists tied to a definite lifestyle. For them, ordinary problems may require very special solutions.

Some of the birds that have been brought here have stayed for just days. One that was knocked down by a cat's paw was unable to lift itself more than a couple of feet from the ground. He was able to fly, but couldn't gain any appreciable altitude. More likely than not, the difficulty was the result of a strained muscle. Three or four days of "R and R" remedied that and he was on his way.

For some, however, it is not that simple and the stay can be prolonged. The length is dictated by the nature of the injury—or when it occurs.

CHARLIE'S STORY

I was not surprised to receive a call early in the 1991 hummingbird season. A local woman's cat had captured an adult male rubythroat two days earlier. She had managed to get the bird away from the cat, but it was injured. The bird was fed some sugar-water with an eyedropper, but wasn't responding—what should she do? We discussed dietary requirements and the bird's absolute need for protein. I suggested that she visit a veterinarian specializing in birds and asked her to let me know of the bird's progress.

When I next spoke with the woman, I was disappointed to learn that no action had yet been taken. She asked if I would take the bird and arranged to deliver him to my office the following morning—five days after his encounter with the cat.

Upon his arrival he appeared generally unkempt, had missing feathers, behaved lethargically, and appeared to be underweight. An appointment was made to visit a veterinarian that afternoon and, more important, the bird was immediately put on a diet of NektarPlus. Charlie, as I had begun to call him, reacted almost instantly to his new diet. As he devoured it, he became much more alert than he had been. For the remainder of that first day Charlie rested on my desk, still in the shoebox in which he had been delivered. He was handfed the nectar every fifteen minutes or so, and at the end of the day, we visited the doctor.

The results of the examination were worse than what I had been expecting. Although the wing wasn't broken, a large piece of tissue was missing from the muscle used to elevate its wing—thus, the bird's inability to fly. Yet that might not be all. Owing to the extent of damage, the soft tissue might be irreparable and, moreover, the doctor was

Charlie

unable to determine whether any additional damage had been done to either the shoulder or the nerves. There was no clue to the bird's future. He suggested that I continue feeding and take a wait-and-see attitude; it might heal on its own. I could tell how badly the doctor felt about this tiniest of patients. He wished me luck and attempted to reassure me with "If anyone can do this, you can."

Charlie was compelled to spend his time in confine-ment. He was placed in an openwork basket instead of the box so he might have a view out. Since keeping him com-fortable but quiet while he was incapacitated was my primary concern, the basket was positioned in such a way that he might have something to look at—a hummingbird feeder at the sunroom window or me at the office. For the first ten days, Charlie accompanied me to work and took the ten-mile ride each way in his stride—except when we'd hit a bump. With each day, he became more alert and active, and within three days of being entrusted to my care, he had regained some of his lost weight. As that first week progressed and Charlie's level of activity increased, he began to maneuver in his basket to reach the feeder secured in the corner on his own. When he wanted to be fed, his tongue would dart in and out and he would attempt to put his wings into motion. If I didn't respond quickly enough, he'd maneuver into position to help himself. It was evident that Charlie was making an effort to regain mobility.

Charlie made repeated attempts to lift himself from the substrate, but with power to only one wing, he could manage merely to go around in circles. When he rested in my hand, wings spread, I could feel a purr—the fluttering movements in his wings as he struggled to do what should ordinarily take no effort at all. Even with all the improvement that he had thus far shown, he would have so much further to go.

Charlie demonstrated a desire for self-maintenance by scraping his beak on a twig, paper towels, or the inside of the feeder tube to clean it, and by making an attempt to preen his right side. His ability to preen effectively had been diminished not only by the injury itself but by a deformity of his right foot, which may have been either a preexisting injury or a life-long deformity. With just a stab at preening, his feathers remained in a rather tousled and scruffy condition and I knew he should have a bath. Because of Squeak's fondness for bathing on a leaf, I tried wetting a large hosta leaf and placing it next to him, hoping that he would use it voluntarily. He showed no interest, so he was helped. I cupped about one tablespoonful of water in my hand and placed him in the little puddle, but he didn't like that, either.

By the end of the second week, Charlie managed to generate about two inches of lift and flew around the bottom of his basket. He engaged in this "flying" repeatedly, and that evening he glided from the palm of my hand to the window screen.

Charlie moved around quite a bit at night—it was too warm and he was too well fed, with good energy reserves, to become torpid. Conditions in the sunroom during the summer season are not controlled, as they had been when Squeak stayed with me, and the windows remained open all day and night. Even when evening temperatures were in the mid-forties, Charlie did not become torpid. He never seemed ready to go to sleep at night and would always wind up rather than down at sunset. Charlie's territory consisted of a small basket. To advertise it, he engaged in head wagging, that side-to-side movement that dominant males perform before retiring for the evening.

June 1, slightly more than two weeks after the incident, was a big day for Charlie. First, he generated enough lift to get himself out of his basket and was sitting on the floor when I walked into the room. Once he became able to do

so, Charlie lifted himself out of the basket over and over
again. Since he frequently landed on the floor, each time I
walked into the sunroom, I had to stop and look around
until I was able to locate him. Each time he was picked up
and placed back in the basket. While there, Charlie was
alert and interested in the hummingbird activity outside.
He was sitting, as he frequently did, staring at a feeder,
waiting for the arrival of the little female that had taken a
fancy to that particular one. Then, when I approached to
offer him some food, he started flying around the room!

Although he was interested in that female, he showed
no interest in chasing her. He wasn't ready for that just yet.
As a matter of fact, when she would look at him, perhaps
instinctively knowing his limitations, he'd turn and look
the other way.

At first Charlie was most cooperative about staying in
his basket, but once he regained some independence,
there was no holding him down. He was not willing to
spend any time in it at all; instead, he wanted to perch on
the skinny branch where Squeak had slept.

For his first night of semi-independence, I wondered
where Charlie would be sleeping and whether he would be
content to stay in the basket when he was placed there for
the evening. Charlie made up his own mind by going to
the basket on his own at retirement time, but that was his
last night of such cooperation. The following night, he
slept in his basket again, but only after I put him there. He
really didn't want to stay and fidgeted and moved around

for quite a while before finally giving in. That was the end of the basket.

When Charlie became more mobile, his feeder was moved from the basket to the shelf, and he was encouraged to fend for himself. Leading a relatively sedentary lifestyle during his recuperation, Charlie consumed approximately 32 milliliters of nectar each day, which consists of water and approximately 3.2 grams of food—roughly equivalent to his body weight, itself close to 3 grams.

In spite of his repeated attempts, the ability to hover independently remained elusive to Charlie for quite some time. Yet he repeatedly tried. When I fed him, he would put his wings into motion while grasping the branch and practice hovering by keeping his good left foot on the perch and raising everything else and spinning his wings. By June 5, he finally managed to hover for several seconds and with each passing day, proficiency increased. He had progressed from a slight purr of his wings to the actual movement of both wings while in a stationary position. This was just going to take time.

When hovering would permit him to visit a hanging feeder, Charlie used that one exclusively rather than the one placed where he might conveniently reach it. He loved his regained ability and hovered constantly. Each time he took a drink, he would fly back to his branch, do a little pirouette, and return for another drink; he frequently exercised his wings while perching.

In less than one month after Charlie's episode with the

cat, he was flying and hovering and vigorously exploring
his surroundings, and it seemed appropriate to have familiar flowers around to alleviate any possible boredom. In
addition to potted plants such as *Bouvardia ternifolia*, fuchsia, *Mimulus cardinalis* and *Hamelia patens*, fresh cuttings of
bee balm (*Monarda* spp.), *Spigelia marilandica*, columbine
(*Aquilegia* spp.), the beloved *Salvia coccinea* and trumpet vine
flowers (*Campsis* spp.) were cut and brought to him daily.
The avid interest that one might expect to be displayed
over such scrumptious offerings was noticeably absent in
Charlie—at least while I was present. When I entered the
sunroom, Charlie would immediately engage in a swallow-
ing action, and his tongue would dart in and out in anticipation and expectation of being fed. When he was alone
in the sunroom, however, he visited his feeders at regular
intervals and investigated all the flowers brought in for
him. He may have been unwilling to do this in my presence, but the telltale dusting of pollen on his crown told
another story: it was a dead giveaway to his activities.
Basically, his private moments were held private, but some
of that private activity was simply obvious. On a number
of occasions when I entered the sunroom he was soaking
wet and his head was loaded with pollen.

While he had been reluctant to bathe on a leaf or in my
hand, and openly disliked being misted, he apparently had
the desire to keep himself clean. The first time that he was
noticeably soaking wet I realized that he had been secretly
visiting the waterfall. Eventually, I was permitted to watch

him bathe. First, he would approach the top pool, where the water flows from the hole in the lava rock and stand on its rim. After allowing the splashes from the running water to hit him for a few seconds, he hopped into the pool and stood in the shallow water, pecking at it. I waited to see if he would lower his body into the water to bathe, but then he continued across the pool and stood directly under the flow—that soaked him. He bathed that way by repeating that action and then abruptly left to dry off.

By June 18, Charlie's hovering had been perfected and the tautness that had been previously noticeable on the injured side was absent. Once physically fit, Charlie finally began showing some real interest in the other hummers, chattering rapidly during their fighting squeals. He wanted to participate, and I knew he was very close to being ready to leave. Not only had he begun chattering and attempting to chase all the other hummers away from the feeders near the windows, he even started to patrol the sunroom. He had truly made the change from total dependence to complete self-sufficiency. His tongue no longer darted in and out in anticipation of being fed when I walked into the room. Now he preferred to do it himself. Although he tolerated me, he wanted no one else on his territory. Charlie was released a few days later. Like Squeak before him, he stopped at the fuchsia and then took off. He followed that irrepressible urge to get back where he belonged—home. And in spite of the maze of directions he had traveled, that urge prevailed. Charlie was an identifiable hummingbird because of his deformed foot and was spotted back on territory, business as usual.

There were many differences between Charlie and Squeak, but the most noticeable was that, as Squeak's stay here progressed, he became more familiar with me and our relationship grew to include many different aspects, whereas as Charlie became more independent, our relationship lessened.

Just a Little Angel Waiting to Get Its Wings

Hummingbirds truly are creatures of the air, and their wings figure prominently in almost all that they do. Because the wings are such an integral part of their very being, when one is injured it is particularly devastating. While other birds can hop from place to place with a pinned and healing wing, not so a hummingbird. These denizens of the air have spindly little feet and legs that are weak and serve little purpose other than for scratching and perching. To get from Point A to Point B, the wings are used.

I don't know the circumstances of this bird's injury. He was just "found" and brought to me after the woman who had found him had been caring for him for several weeks. The bird was alert and responsive, but as a result of an apparent shoulder injury, wing feathers—more so on the injured side—and the tips of most of the tail feathers had broken off. The bird was so tiny. I realized that hummingbirds truly defy the principles of distance and perception, for the closer one gets, the smaller they seem.

The minute I saw him, he peeped—not just once, but over and over again. So often that I said, "My, you're quite a little peeper." I never really gave him a name; as after that I would greet him by saying, "Hello, Little Peeper." But more often than not I referred to him as Munchkin, the Little Angel or, mostly, My Little Problem Child.

Their almost rudimentary feet and legs mean a special set of problems is created in caring for injured hummingbirds. With broken wing feathers, this bird would be unable to fly and any attempt by him to do so could worsen his situation. For with just small bits of feather shafts remaining, the wing became vulnerable to direct damage that might make the wing unable to grow *any* feathers. He would have to be confined to a basket and kept as immobile as possible until his injury was healed and the broken wing feathers replaced during his first full molt, which might take at least until spring. Squeak never went through a complete molt, and I've always wondered about the photoperiod and what affect it may have on hormones that initiate feather replacement. This time it would be imperative that I do whatever necessary to encourage a molt, so I provided a maximum of only eleven hours of artificial lighting and allowed the sun to lengthen that time naturally as days became longer.

Being confined for so long could lead to boredom and frustration, and constant perching could create problems for Peeper's legs or feet. He was kept in a small basket lined on its insides with foam as a buffer to protect his wing. The bottom was covered with soft, six-ply paper toweling—soft enough to minimize damage to the wing should he fall but not so soft that his claws would get caught. A feeder was placed in the basket, as was a perch. The perch would have to be low enough for him to get up without using his beak as a "third foot," as they are inclined to do, but since hummingbirds perch best in a vertical position, it would have to be high enough for him to be comfortable.

Confinement and restriction were an absolute necessity if he were to heal and recover his flying abilities, but his problems were exacerbated by their remedy. Most solutions to his myriad problems seemed to fit into that "damned if you do, damned if you don't" category. For instance, any time I picked him up, unless it was an emergency, I scrupulously washed and thoroughly rinsed and dried my hands. Human skin has oils, acids, and other properties that might damage a hummingbird's feathers. Yet I *had* to pick him up. Gloves can't be used, no matter how thin, as you must be able to feel the claws from *both* feet before you lift. I would get my fingers underneath him and nudge a bit until he put his feet on me so as not to lift while they were clinging to something else. Since I picked him up roughly every fifteen minutes to change the padding in his basket, I tried to make that pleasant for him by also taking him to the window to look out or to some flowers for some real nectar.

For a tiny bird Peeper was quite a handful! He was his

Visiting flowers for real nectar

own worst enemy and not very patient with himself. He refused to accept his limitations and had quite a knack for getting himself into trouble. Occasionally his beak would penetrate the foam that lined his basket to about $\frac{1}{64}$ inch, but he did not struggle to free himself—although he could have done so with ease. He was very cautious about that beak and wouldn't take any chances with it. Instead, he would sit as still as could be and wait for help. I was always nearby to pull the foam back. And each time he would get himself into trouble by falling off his perch, I would help him get back up so he wouldn't damage anything. Then, as soon as he would have both feet back on the perch and be in position to drink, he'd chirp as if to say, "I've got it."

But he wasn't doing that well. I couldn't keep him out of trouble no matter how hard I tried, and nothing I did seemed to help. It was as if we were always taking two steps forward and one step back or one step forward and two steps back. There were days full of tears of frustration over my inability to keep him immobile enough that he wouldn't hit his wing. And there were days when I questioned my own motives. I wasn't placing this burden only on myself; he was bearing the brunt of it. But when I talked to him, he "talked back" with his little peeps, or he'd stretch first one wing and then the other, enjoying my attention. He wasn't an unhappy bird, and I wanted to give him a chance. But there was something else that kept me going: when he would spin his wings, they showed the same pattern and range of motion as any normal hummingbird and I knew that when his right wing got new feathers, he'd fly.

All it takes is just one little thing to turn the tide. Finally, one day I found the key that began to unlock the secrets to a smooth recovery. The inherent nature of close confinement made the daily bath an absolute necessity. On sunny days when solar warmth promoted speedy drying, Peeper frequently had more than one bath. But even on dismal days it was very important to keep him clean. As a confined bird, the chance of getting soiled feathers or having food drip on him was much greater. So when weather conditions were not conducive to rapid, natural drying, I'd use the hairdryer, held far enough away and never directed near the eyes. But his feathers were gradually losing something and one day, in spite of the sun, he just wasn't drying quickly enough. Fearful that he might be susceptible to respiratory problems, I thought it best to intervene. "A little feather-fluffing will do it," I thought as I reached for a small makeup brush.

I have been very surprised by some of the things I've seen hummingbirds do—most notable of which was the strength exhibited by Rosie when she lifted an entire piece of material three or four inches from a chair by a single fiber. But nothing I had seen thus far had prepared me for what I would see next. If I hadn't seen it for myself, surely I would never have believed it. I've always had to pick this bird up to change the padding at the bottom of his basket. He didn't like it and would shrink from my hand, but I had no other choice. While it was heartrending to see him cringe from me, there was no other way—he and his surroundings *had* to be kept clean. This time I picked him up and held him against my abdomen with my hand cupped lightly around him. With the small makeup brush, I began to lift and fluff his throat feathers to dry them off. He seemed to enjoy what I was doing and lifted his head, making access easier. Lifting against the grain, I ran the brush up from his breast to under his beak. The more I did that, the more content he became. I fluffed his cheek feathers and he closed his eyes; I fluffed his neck and he lifted his head. I was getting all the places he couldn't scratch because of his balance difficulties.

Peeper enjoyed this scratching so much I decided to have these preening sessions more often. To start, he would lie against my abdomen while I kept my hand cupped around him as he rested his head on the inside of my thumb. I could even feel the warm, spent air from his nasal passage. Occasionally he'd rub his beak and the side of his face on my thumb, or he'd check out little pieces of cuticle or flaking skin too small for me to notice. He'd start by sitting erect, but once I began fluffing his chin, he would lean to his side a tad. Then as I preened his side, he would lift his wing and the next thing I knew, he really began to list. Before long, he would roll over on his back and totally enjoy having his undersides done. When I'd fluff under his wing, he'd raise it. When I preened the side of his face, he'd close his eyes. But it was when I preened his throat that he was in ecstacy. He'd stretch his neck and open and close his eyes the way a cat does when it feels such pleasure. The only thing he didn't do was purr. He enjoyed it so much that at times he appeared to drift off to sleep while I preened him. Since drying him this way proved to be so welcome, I reasoned that it might also be the best way to bathe him. Initially I'd make a cup with my palm and create a little puddle to stick him in—after all, it was the underparts primarily that needed the water—but with the brush I could concentrate on the feathers that needed it most. And so, his grooming sessions became two parts—wash and dry.

There were two brushes that I would use during grooming. The first was a sable artist's brush dipped in water to clean his feathers, particularly the ones around his face where there might be food residue; the second was the small makeup brush for fluffing and preening. And he knew the difference between them. He loved to rub his beak all over the wet bathing brush and liked me to lie it on my thumb so he could rub his chin and throat over it until he was so wet that he looked like a hatchling—perhaps one-half the size of a fluffed-out hummer. He was so small and cute in an ugly sort of way, scrawny looking, with his tiny head sitting on his skinny little neck. He reminded me of a chick just out of its egg. I tried to compare his tiny body to some other familiar object—all I could come up with was an almond.

Peeper would inspect the brush, sticking his beak through its bristles, and every once in a while he'd open his mouth and try to bite it. When he'd grab it, he'd invariably give it a shake or two in that side-to-side motion typical of a puppy. He'd bite it, grab it, pull it, and shake it. Then he'd rub his face on the brush and want to hold its tip with his foot while he made an attempt to rub it all over the rest of him. At least once during each session he would have to explore the brush, poking his beak in between the bristles and sticking out his tongue. With a $1/16$-inch-diameter, soft but strong and dense Kolinsky red sable brush, I could easily lift and fluff his tiniest feathers—the minuscule ones jutting out under the mandible—and even separate and fluff the downy feathers around his legs and his bottom. He loved it. After several minutes of preening, his feathers would suddenly become fluffy and he would look like a hummingbird again. His feathers were kept so soft and fluffy that his throat and breast looked like soft fur. What had started out as a way to make sure he was dry turned into a ritual. Hummingbirds don't engage in mutual preening, but I'll bet if they did, they would love it.

After that, when I would stick my hand in his basket to lift him out, he no longer cringed but practically jumped into my hand—that is, if he didn't explore my cuticle with his tongue instead. He expected me to preen him each time

The only thing he didn't do was purr

I lifted him out of the basket, so even when I was only changing his pad and hadn't planned to, I'd make it my business to brush him at least a little bit. Prior to that there was only one thing I could do that kept him happy and quiet: to have him sit in my hand and look out the window. He loved looking out, his little head would move this way and that, as he'd look up at the trees. He never squirmed or made any attempt to get away from me. He was truly content and seemed almost mesmerized by what was out there. His enjoyment of our newfound physical relationship made a tremendous difference in all aspects of his recovery, and now he wanted to be held all the time—either in my cupped hand or hanging on my T-shirt, where he would cling like a little woodpecker on a tree trunk. It kept him out of trouble, so that's what I did—I held him constantly.

As time passed, it became progressively more difficult to keep Peeper's feathers clean. They weren't drying rapidly because they were no longer *really* clean or protected by his preening oil. Food undoubtedly was the culprit. The NektarPlus is sticky, and it was difficult to keep it away from his feathers under such close circumstances. Water was no longer sufficient and as occasional slightly sticky feathers dried, they'd mat down on his skin here and there, probably pulling it. I had to think of something else. I found myself pondering the problem over and over in my mind. What could I clean him with? It is not only the feathers I would have to be concerned with—I didn't want to use anything that would irritate his skin. I was reluctant to try anything that hadn't been used on hummingbirds before, being unwilling to experiment. The only thing I could think of as a possibility was Dawn dish detergent. While I am unaware of its use on hummingbirds, I know it as the product used to clean birds caught in oil slicks. But first I would try to get an experienced opinion, if possible.

I called the Arizona-Sonora Desert Museum, as there is a hummingbird aviary there, and I hoped to speak with someone who could advise me whether or not to try this. Unfortunately I missed the return call. It was Friday and I didn't want to put it off for the weekend, so I went against conventional wisdom. After much soul-searching, I nervously made a bold decision to try it. I was afraid to use any more than just the smallest amount of detergent. I just touched it with my finger and then swished my finger around in a plastic film container of warm water. To test it, I took the brush and cleaned his uppertail coverts. These feathers don't lie directly on the skin and thus provided a good starting point. I could examine the result and determine whether it would be safe—or worth it—to continue. I then rinsed them well with warm water and dried them. The feathers were beautiful! It was working! When I saw how successful I had been, I was encouraged to be more thorough. I did all the feathers, section by section, stopping to rinse and check his skin. Then I absorbed what water I could with a paper towel and Q-Tips before proceeding to fluff him dry. We spent a couple of hours at this project, but when I was finished, his feathers looked great—green, shiny, and fluffy. I was so pleased and he was, too. With no feathers pulling at his skin, he was comfortable and happy. It was obvious that he felt better and he was beautiful. It was a success.

On Monday morning I received the call from a man at the museum. I told him what I had done and why. Ordinarily, he said, he wouldn't recommend it, but all things considered, I had probably done the best thing for him. Then he gave me one other bit of advice, something that might help with his molt. Because Peeper was a relatively inactive bird, he probably ate less than the others. I suppose that is true, although I had never measured food intake. When birds are active, they drink more frequently, converting sugars into quick energy that is burned during their constant comings and goings. NektarPlus contains 2.9 percent protein, which is stored. Constant feeding means more protein intake overall. Inactive birds need and drink less nectar and thus are taking in less total protein overall. But protein is needed for feather replacement, and an inactive bird consuming a diet formulated for active birds would need additional protein to compensate. He suggested that a pinch of high-protein flaked fish food be added to his feeder, which I promptly purchased. Analysis on the fish food container indicated 47 percent protein.

Once the preening sessions began and Peeper decided he liked sitting in my hand best of all places, I began holding him for extended periods to keep him happy and out of trouble. Almost immediately I noticed a remarkable improvement. He liked the warmth of my hand, he no longer hit his wing, his feet were no longer sore and in fact had regained their strength—he would clasp the skin of my hand with his prickly little claws and I could feel the difference. And after his feathers were cleaned with the Dawn, he became more comfortable and more active.

The consensus is that hummers shouldn't be held—it's too stressful for them. With this bird, however, the opposite proved to be his salvation. It changed his increasing problems into steady progress. He'd snuggle in my slightly cupped hand just the way a bird might sit on eggs in a nest, and he was content. He liked the warmth and, I believe, the texture of my skin. He'd exercise his wings while sitting in my hand just the way a juvenile in a nest might do, and he'd raise his body either by stretching his legs or pushing his beak into my palm while twirling his wings. He loved being preened and he loved looking out the window or lying in the sun when the rays hit him. He'd dip way over on his side so his skin could soak in the warmth. I could even see a difference when I took him to visit flowers. Now he actively bounced from one to the next. He felt well and he enjoyed life.

Peeper may have been feeling quite well, but he was nowhere near being out of the woods. We had managed to get him to the position where the wing was the only problem and then maintain the status quo, but our biggest challenge waited just around the corner. The wing feathers are sequentially replaced from the inside outward except that the ninth is skipped and is replaced after the tenth.* This would mean that as new wing feathers grew in, there would be no old outer feathers to protect them. They would be subject to direct damage. I figured that I might as well get used to holding him because the better he felt, the more active he would become. When his wing feathers started to grow in, that activity might cause them to break off. But we were on the right track and had finally hit just the right combination of variables.

Having a more intimate relationship with this bird than I've had with any other has opened much more to observation than I had previously and has revealed many new glimpses into the private lives of hummingbirds that had heretofore been secret—at least to me. For example, Peeper drank frequently during the day, having many sips before going to sleep, several of which he would take after the lights went out but while there was still enough ambient light; at times he would drink so much that the swollen crop stood out like a sore thumb. He urinated just as frequently but he never urinated overnight, and his pad, which was changed for the last time each day just as the lights went out, would be dry in the morning. Then, when he did urinate in the morning, the concentration was especially strong. That tells me that overnight either his body

---

*Primary feathers are numbered 1 to 10, starting at the inside—closest to the body—and working outward to the leading edge of the wing. There are ten tail feathers (rectrices), or five pairs. The pairs are numbered from the center outward, the middle pair being the first and the outermost, the fifth.

used the water portion of the nectar in some other way or he lost it in some way other than urination—perhaps evaporation. What convinced me that the latter was the most likely was that he was noticeably lighter in the mornings. I didn't weigh him, but he felt like "nothing" in the morning, whereas during the afternoon I could feel a certain heaviness that seemed to be centered at his bottom.

When I tried to look at the tip of his wing through a magnifying glass, Peeper became extremely frightened as, from his perspective, my already large eyes became grotesque.

The uropygial gland is located at the base of the tail. This gland, also called the "preening gland," secretes an oil used to waterproof and maintain the feathers. On his "good days," while sitting in my hand, he would try to preen and I was able to get a bird's-eye view of the procedure. He would position his beak at the base of the gland (closest to his body), and with the little cone-shaped protuberance in between the upper and lower sections of his beak, he would squeeze his beak and pull it toward the tip. So instead of just touching his beak to the gland, he would squeeze the substance out. When *I* preened him, I would touch the brush to his preening gland, too. I hoped that would be beneficial to his feathers and an improvement over just the brush, but I don't know if it made any difference.

Peeper was the only hummingbird that has stayed with me to become torpid at night, and it only happened on a couple of occasions. But torpidity wasn't entered immediately, for he would move around in his basket during the evening—and had done so at least a couple of times on the nights before becoming torpid—but he was torpid in the morning. That indicates to me that hummingbirds can become torpid at any time if energy reserves dip below a certain point. It took him between ten and fifteen minutes in a warm hand to revive.

There probably has been no hummingbird in avian history that has been held, preened or pampered as much as Peeper. But he may have an insurmountable combination of problems and so I don't know if he'll make it. Certainly the deck seems stacked against him. But once I discovered the key to keeping him happy, clean, healthy, and injury free, his future began to look brighter. The rest is a matter of time. He is just a little angel, waiting to get his wings.

K-T—MY LITTLE MIRACLE BIRD

While returning from lunch, Kate Scheffel, a dispatcher from the police department, found something lying on the ground in front of the bank's plate glass window. At first she thought it was a bug, then quickly realized that it was a hummingbird—but it appeared to be dead. When she took a second look, however, she could detect breathing and discovered that the bird was indeed alive. Apparently it had flown into the window and took a direct hit at full speed. Kate picked up the pitiful little body, returned to the desk, and called me. "Is this Hummingbirds 911?" As luck would have it, my husband George, a police officer, was on duty at the time and transported the bird to me posthaste.

George arrived with the bird within minutes, but it appeared that it might not have long to live. The base of the mandible was pushed quite far out at the left side and upper and lower portions of the beak were crisscrossed. In addition, the entire side and part of the top of its head was swollen and misshapen. And the bird was unconscious. Undoubtedly there was a severe concussion.

The sight of this poor broken and dying little bird was heartbreaking, and I had to decide what to do, as the injury looked as though it must be painful. First I placed a call to the veterinary college at Cornell, as one man there has done a little work with hummingbirds. I wanted an experienced opinion on whether there was *any* hope. I waited and waited for a call back. Finally, while I was waiting, the bird opened its eyes a bit—it was beginning to regain consciousness. All this time I had been holding the bird in my hand to keep it warm. Once the eyes opened, I tried to feed it. While it made no effort to eat, when some of the NektarPlus touched its tongue, the bird instinctively went through the motions. But the food just bubbled out the side of the beak where it was out of line, and the tongue flailed about wildly, since it was not following its normal "track." After several hours, the bird regained full consciousness and attempted to eat when fed, but the food still dripped out and down the side of its throat. The bird also began to move its wings but still looked absolutely

As K-T visits stachys, the injury to the healing beak is visible

K-T's throat was only very faintly streaked, a female characteristic

Leaves of zebra plant
(Aphelandra squarrosa) *are a good place to bathe . . .*

. . . and the flowers are a good source of nectar

awful. It couldn't keep its balance and flopped over when I
tried to get it to sit up. When it was time to put the bird
to sleep for the night, I placed a branch for grasping across
the bottom of the bird's basket and circled the bird with
rolled-up paper towel "bumpers," as it couldn't hold itself
up. The basket was then placed side by side with Peeper's
basket so they could sleep next to one another.

I waited all day for the veterinarian's call back, all the
while worried that the bird might be suffering, but the call
wouldn't come until the next day. Now I'm glad that it
took so long, for the next morning I was surprised to see
that the bird's beak had moved back into place just a bit
—certainly not where it belonged, barely noticeable yet
less pronounced. The food still dribbled out when it was
fed, and I had to bathe the face with a sable watercolor
brush frequently lest the feathers rot off its face. The bird
had no trouble grasping a perch but continued to be
unable to maintain its balance and couldn't keep itself
upright unless the wings were in motion. If the bird tried
to stop its wings, it would flop over until hanging upside
down and then stay that way. But the minute progress that
was evident by the next morning indicated there might be
some hope.

There are several ways to determine the gender
of immature rubythroats. Probably the most noticeable
characteristics, at least in the field, are throat and tail patterns. Immature males tend to be darker overall and have
throats (often with some iridescent red feathers) that are

more or less heavily streaked. Females' throats are only faintly streaked, if streaked at all. Females have more white on the outer three tail feathers (Rectrices 3 to 5) than males, and often there is a small amount of white on Rectrix 2 (next to middle), as well.

Finally, when sexing a bird in hand, the shape of certain wing feathers are conclusive. While the inner six primaries are much narrower than the outer four, the sixth primary itself (fifth, counting from the outside) is much narrower on males. The tapered, outer web is virtually nonexistent in males, whereas it is at least 1 millimeter wide throughout in females.

The wings never stopped moving, so it was difficult to make an irrefutable identification based upon that character. However, the throat had no iridescent red feathers and was only very faintly streaked. In fact, the bird later replaced throat feathers with even whiter ones. The bird was a little dark around the edges, but based on the throat it seemed obvious that it was a female. Being more interested in the bird's condition than its gender, I made a snap mental identification and then forgot about it.

Later, quite by accident, I noticed that the sixth primary showed evidence of belonging to a male, but I still had that contradictory, snow-white throat staring me right in the face. What was going on here? Wear and tear might have shaved off an edge, but examination revealed that the right and left sides were alike. It appeared that bird was a male. Although that convinced me of the bird's sex, when the tail ultimately began its molt, I anticipated the final verifying word on gender. Then, once it began and just after the two middle pairs of tail feathers were pushed out, I noticed the tiniest, most minute iridescent red speck near the edge of the throat. Under advantageous lighting, it stood out just as though a tiny red sparkle had fallen off a Christmas card, landed on the bird, and burrowed down until it was nestled among the feathers of this otherwise snowy-white throat—ever so tiny but ever so present. The rubythroat was a male indeed and the wings didn't lie. Once I had made that initial determination, it just never occurred to me to verify gender later by examining the wings. The information was available to me—the signs were all there—but I neglected to use it. That was my mistake, and I think it goes without saying that I shall never make such a mistake again.

The bird would have to have a name and the *only* appropriate name for this lucky little bird would be some form of Katie—Kate Scheffel's namesake. But when I determined that Katie was a he, the name was changed. K-T was a good choice: first, the initials appropriately stand for King Tut, his very best behavioral trait and, of course, he would still be named after Kate.

To keep his feathers clean, especially when food dripped, K-T received a spray bath every day. But since he was not yet self-sufficient, I had to dry him with a hair-dryer, held away from his eyes and at a distance from his body. I just wanted enough warmish air to dry him off, not dry him out. Each day K-T showed a little more improvement. I continued to hand-feed him and hold him periodically but frequently to give his wings a rest; if he became tired and stopped, he still flopped. Eventually he was able to stop his wings without flopping all the way over. He'd sit up, sort of wrapped around the perch. Then, as he became tired, the little semicircle of his body became tighter and tighter as he tried to combat the slipping that he apparently felt—until, when it reached its maximum I suppose, his wings would go into motion, he'd straighten himself up, and start again.

After several days, K-T was able to feed himself from the feeder—and oh, what a voracious appetite he had! He still dribbled a bit, still slept later than Little Peeper, and still had a bit of a balance problem, but he was improving. K-T had not vocalized at all and that, too, had been a concern to me. Could it be a sign of some other problem—not external and therefore not visible? Finally, after he had been here several days, I heard one weak chirp in the morning. It wasn't a conversation, but it *was* a start. To help with his balance, I made him a "donut"—a small semicircle made from a pipe cleaner and attached at an upward angle to his perch. This gave him something to brace himself against and he had a double perch in front of the feeder to serve the same purpose—they would stop him from flopping over as much. The device worked pretty well, but he had to be watched constantly. After about a week, he was able to perch while sleeping and, instead of being placed

K-T inspects water droplets before bathing

. . . then he wets his chin

. . . his breast

. . . and his abdomen

at the bottom of the basket surrounded by the bumpers, he slept normally. He still used the double perch and I checked him repeatedly. I was afraid that if he flopped over, he might land on his beak. And I no longer had to use a hair dryer after his bath.

Eventually K-T was graduated from the basket to a "halfway house," a small screened enclosure where he could practice limited flying, landing, and probing flowers. After a few days, when he appeared to be doing reasonably well, he was given free rein in the sunroom. He still had a bit of a balance problem; occasionally he would start to fall and then straighten up, and he still had difficulty lifting his foot to scratch without using his wings to maintain balance. It wouldn't be until November that he *would* be able to scratch. He still slept a wee bit later than the other hummer, and his face was still just a little screwed up, but all things considered, he was doing so well. I didn't know if his beak would ever be 100 percent, but he had begun to make a remarkable recovery and, while he was nowhere near strong enough to make a migration, I anticipated being able to release my little "miracle bird" in the spring.

There is a positive side to everything. If this had to happen to him at all, it occurred at the best possible of times, during his fall migration while he was carrying extra weight. K-T was more than chubby; he was fat and had gained weight in all the usual places—rump, back of neck, throat, and belly. This was helpful to him in two ways: the first and most obvious would be reserves to help him through a period of reduced food and possible body temperature inadequacies; the second was his speed, which may have been reduced by one-third to one-half of his average 27 to 30 mph, as a result of carrying that additional weight. Crashing at 15 or 20 mph instead of 30 probably saved his life. Although he lost some of the weight he carried with him upon his arrival, he still retained too much of it—he was obese for a hummingbird. He would be leading a sedentary lifestyle, particularly while recovering, so his obesity was a concern to me. I certainly couldn't put him on a diet. What he really needed was activity. He needed to burn off that extra weight.

Once K-T was released from the halfway house to the sunroom, his true personality began to emerge, and he turned out to be unlike any other hummer. Although I feel it is best to handle the birds as infrequently as possible, there are circumstances when that is not always an option —and so it was with K-T. Perhaps because I worked so closely with him, he had become accustomed to me. Maybe he was more trusting and friendly naturally; maybe he just liked me. But he treated me as no other hummer ever has, and he quickly wormed his way into my heart.

A 400-watt high-intensity grow lamp shielded by protective glass replaced the fluorescents of old in the sunroom. This was an improvement in efficiency and took up less space. It also generated more heat and the hummers are fond of that. When I would hold my hand under the

K-T positioned himself between me and the lemon flowers to drink nectar

The mother resumed the care of her chicks

Little One was an adorable little nestling—note the pollen on her beak

Flowers were Little One's learning tools—bee balm (Monarda)

light, K-T would fly up and sit on it and just bask in some beloved warmth. He was fearless. When I realized just how much he liked it, I knew it was incumbent upon me to provide something more permanent than my hand. A small bare branch stuck in a container of sand gave him a place to sit about eighteen inches below the light. But that wasn't enough. He might want to sit closer, so I rearranged some plants and dragged the trusty old honeysuckle over to where several either fresh or old branches would reach out at various levels under the light. Now he could be as close or far away as his fancy dictated. Of course, once I provided some natural sitting places, my hand was out of the picture. Sure, he was the typical little "user," but he obviously trusted me since he was willing to sit on my hand, crane his neck all the way to the side, open his wing, and give himself up completely to the light's warmth.

It was hard not to fall in love with K-T when he would do some of the things he did. Once I was on my hands and knees, picking up some dried-up blossoms, leaves, and dust with a small brush and dustpan when I heard someone hovering behind my head. All of a sudden he was in front of my eyes, looking as though to say, "What are you doing?" Next, I could feel him hovering over my head again, around and around, and then, finally, he sat on the top of my head in my hair. When I would do things at Peeper's basket, K-T would hover around my hands and inspect, touching my fingers with his tongue and exploring the folds in my skin where the fingers bend at the knuckles. He was outgoing and personable, nosy and brazen. When I changed the water in the waterfall, he would immediately come over to investigate. Even though he never chose to take advantage of the waterfall for bathing purposes, he could obviously relate it to bathing. The minute I would busy myself in his vicinity, K-T would inspect the gardenia leaves that I would wet down for him to bathe on. We—meaning K-T and I—had tried other places for bathing, such as the cattleya leaves, but they dried off too quickly. He liked both barleria leaves and those of the zebra plant (*Aphelandra squarrosa*), but the gardenia was his favorite—maybe because of the angle of the leaves, or maybe because there are so many more leaves altogether, or maybe no reason at all except that he just liked it. Since the gardenia was his obvious favorite, that was what he would have.

At the very least, K-T was insatiably curious about everything I did. He'd buzz around my head until I removed the feeder from where it was hung and hand-feed him. He preferred getting the food from me even though I only took his own feeder down to do it. I wondered why. When I would go over to the lemon tree to get a whiff of its fragrant flowers, K-T would immediately come over to inspect and then position himself between my nose and the blossom to drink the nectar—so brazen and absolutely adorable. One day he boldly hovered right up under my chin to get the embroidered flowers outlining the collar on my shirt. He was totally trusting and absolutely fearless, and I knew it would be extremely difficult to sever my relationship with him come spring.

LITTLE ONE

There are times when some advice and perhaps just a smidgen of help will do the trick. Take, for instance, the call that came regarding a rubythroat's nest built on a well-rotted oak branch that had blown down during a thunderstorm—with its occupants intact. The nest, still attached to its original anchor, was tied up in the same tree that had hosted it originally and was placed as closely as possible to its original location. After that, the wait began to see if the mother would return to resume the care of her chicks. By next morning, she had begun to care for them again and continued to do so until they fledged.

Some aren't that lucky. There are times when little nestlings just can't be put back. Take, for instance, the Little One. In late July I had a call from a woman who had found a baby hummingbird. The municipal highway department from a nearby town had been pruning some tree branches and while feeding the clippings into a chipper, discovered the chick on the ground. No one knows what happened to the nest or the other nestling; I make the assumption that the nest contained the standard two occupants. If left there, surely the chick would have died—the mother was nowhere in sight nor did she turn up later. The absolutely adorable nestling, still with a short and thick reddish-orange beak, short picket-fence tail, and small wings, all characteristic of a nestling, was brought to me for care until it would be ready to fledge.

Feeling right at home, Little One perched on my hand, drank some NektarPlus, and then cleaned her beak by wiping it back and forth across my finger. The bird sat outside with me each day and, growing at a remarkable rate, looked less like a nestling and more like a fledgling with each passing day. And the day quickly came that Little One, after having spent several days exercising her wings, raised herself up a couple of feet to a low branch of the spruce tree. After that, she stayed in the sunroom on a branch of the ficus that I borrowed from my Mom—now that the bird was moving about there would be no stopping her. When she showed signs of being on the road to self-sufficiency, her feeder was placed in the ficus and she was encouraged to use her own resources; she learned in no time flat. During this mock fledgling period, Little One should learn about flowers. Potted plants were bought for the garden—new salvia, bee balm, lobelia, spider flower, flowering tobacco. All would be planted outside ultimately, but for now they would be Little One's learning tools. I wanted to introduce her to favorite hummingbird flowers that she might encounter on her long, ultimate trip south. Before I released her I would introduce her to different feeders as well.

There's one thing I've learned about hummingbirds: as they move from one chapter in their lives to the next, they never look back. As usual, I was apprehensive about

releasing Little One—and hesitant. All the typical moth-
erly fears—outside, alone, overnight . . . maybe she'd like
to come back in for the night. I would have no trouble
should she come right over to me and perch on my finger.
Was she *really* ready? Would she stay around long enough
to show me that she truly was able to care for herself?
Concerns aside, it was time. Well, I did it—I brought her
out and released her. To my delight, she basically stayed
right near me all day. I continued to hand-feed her, and in
between she visited flowers close by or perches five or six
feet away. I finally released a hummingbird that didn't
leave me flat!

But "never looking back" means staying out all night,
whether I liked it or not. She was the last hummer to leave
that first evening—and each evening after. She slept in the
spruce tree, on a skinny branch two or three feet above the
overhang behind the sunroom. She looked so small, she
was all alone, and I felt sad. But I was relieved to know her
location. I was up before the sun the next morning and
before coffee or anything else, I went outside to see if she
was still there and check her condition. I was relieved
when I was able to detect her silhouette (only because I
had already known her location) and determine that she
had made it through the night. Being the closest to the
house, Little One was the first hummer to arrive at the
feeder the next morning. But she didn't visit an ordinary
feeder—she flew right over to me and hovered eye-to-
eye with me, buzzed around my hand, and then got right

back "in my face" and peeped. She was demanding some
food. I loved it. I had her feeder in hand just in case and
immediately gave her what she wanted. She expected me
to be there, feeder in hand, at all times and when she
wanted to be fed, she'd sail up to my eyes and insist.

For the next few days, Little One didn't venture more
than ten or fifteen feet away from the fledging spot, just
outside of the sunroom. She visited flowers, lobelia and
cannas, but in between would sail over to my hand to be
fed. When I wasn't holding the feeder, she'd be right up at
my face, demanding.

Before long, Little One began to venture farther away
and made forays to the different flower patches throughout the garden. And she'd sit on one of the hummingbird
branches that I have scattered here and there and watch
the other young hummingbirds. They moved quickly and
obviously fascinated her. Before long she succumbed to a
strong natural urge and began to chase them. She was
brazen and totally fearless with the other hummers, and
she seemed determined to let everyone, young and old,
know that she had arrived on the scene.

Eventually, Little One became totally self-sufficient.
She used all the feeders, explored all the hummingbird
flowers, captured insects, and fit into the hummingbird
community in that bratty hummingbird way. She had
loads of personality. Everyone who met her fell in love
with her instantly—the way she would fearlessly sail in,
inspect the hand, fly up to the face, and peeping up a

storm, demand some food. She made herself absolutely and totally irresistible. But as would be expected, that behavior was short-lived. Eventually she began sleeping elsewhere, and I wasn't privy to that location. And instead of begging me for food, I'd have to take the food over to where she sat and beg her to take it. I didn't want to lose that aspect of our relationship—it was special to me—but Little One didn't care about that because eventually she discontinued that, too. Oh, she'd sail up to my face and peep, but that was it. She'd sail up, peep, and then go off chasing something or using the "big" hummingbird feeders. She stayed around, eventually fattened up, and about mid-September left for parts unknown. She was born on the other side of the river, but she fledged from my sunroom. The mystery is: to which will she return in the spring—the birth or fledging site? Unfortunately, I won't recognize her unless she sails up to my face and peeps at me.

THE RUFOUS INVASION

My father spent a lot of time on the road during the 1930s. Depression-era America was a different time, a time when one could travel across this country or south as far as Panama, working a day or two here and there and then moving on, seeing everything in a way that just can't be done today, more than sixty years later. I can recall many of the interesting stories he had told me of his life on the road during that time, but the one that stands out most vividly is of one woman in Louisiana who had many beautiful flowers on her porch or balcony to attract hummingbirds. "Look at the birds," she said to my father as she pointed out a number of hummers working the blossoms.

"And," my father remembered, "there were different kinds there—some were different colors; one was reddish." No doubt he had seen a rufous hummingbird.

This is obviously not something brand-new to the hospitable Southeast. A number of documented rufous hummingbirds regularly winter there. Some banded individuals practicing what is known as winter site fidelity have returned several years in a row. In fact, several species of hummingbird, none of which are considered eastern birds, now winter in the Gulf coastal area. The Northeast is quite another story.

RUFOUS PIONEERS

For years the rufous was considered strictly a western bird, but with a tendency to wander during its southward fall migration. The status of the rufous in the Southeast—particularly along the Gulf Coast—eventually graduated from casual (occurring infrequently in a geographic area) to vagrant (occurring outside its normal range usually during or following migration). Through banding efforts of people such as Nancy Newfield and Bob Sargent, we now know that the Southeast has become a major wintering ground for perhaps hundreds of rufous hummingbirds. So while the rufous became more recognized as a regular visitor (or migrant) to southeastern states, it was still considered accidental, or occurring infrequently farther north. Recently, however, there has been an explosion of rufous hummingbirds in the Northeast. Have they been around for a long

time and we are just noticing them more now that we keep
our feeders up longer in the fall? Or are we witnessing pioneers of this species expanding their range and settling in
new places? Perhaps both are correct. There has probably
been a range expansion effort in progress for quite a while,
but it is really beginning to gather momentum. And being
more hummingbird oriented, we are noticing them more
now. This phenomenon may not be restricted to the rufous,
but certainly that is the most common out-of-range species
in the eastern United States. It has become our second
most common Eastern hummingbird!

If a new or expanded wintering range is evolving, what
about a correspondingly expanded breeding range? Did
that already occur when the rufous moved into Alaska, or
was Alaska just the start of what will ultimately include the
Northeast as well? In *Netlines*, the Hummer/Bird Study
Group newsletter,* Bob Sargent relates that rufous hummingbirds have been documented in every month of the
year except June in the Southeast. Why—what is going
on? Who knows. It is a nagging, thought-provoking question, and the possible answers are many. With thousands
upon thousands of individual hummingbirds of many
species either year-round residents of or wintering in
Mexico, it is immediately obvious that competition would

*For more information, or for those interested in participating, contact Hummer/
Bird Study Group, Inc., P.O. Box 250, Clay, Alabama 35048-0250. Another organization is The Hummingbird Society. Dedicated to hummingbird conservation
and research, the organization has an impressive scientific advisory board and pub-
lishes a quarterly newsletter. For information about joining, call (800) 529-3699.

be keener on traditional wintering grounds. Conditions in traditional wintering areas may have become—or are becoming—unfavorable. The balance between the number of competitors and the amount of available food may have changed—perhaps the result of habitat destruction not only on the wintering ground but also in nearby areas. That may have increased the concentration of residents, transients, and migrants into smaller areas. I certainly don't know; I can only speculate about the possibilities. The one thing I am sure of is that the status of the rufous hummingbird east of its purported range has changed. We can guess and speculate to our hearts' content, but there's so much that we just don't know. With each new bit of information, however, another piece of the puzzle drops into place, and one day maybe we *will* know.

As mentioned, this change may be occurring to compensate for added breeding areas to the north, a northward shift to cut down on travel time. Certainly the rufous spends a lot of time traveling, and for a great deal of its time it is en route somewhere. There are many people who never travel as far in their entire lifetime as the rufous travels on its migration—and they do it *twice* each year. Birds and other animals will expand or change their range in response to environmental pressures and other factors to better accommodate their needs. The basic needs for breeding and nonbreeding hummingbirds are flowers and insects. So the hospitality of, say, a Louisiana garden brimming with flowers and feeders means more time for the important stuff in life. The rufous breeds in some areas where the brevity of the flowering season restricts it to one brood per year. Perhaps this is part of an effort to extend the breeding season in some way so more offspring can be produced in additional broods.

Is this "explosion" a result of external factors, or is it internal? When weather patterns are examined, the increase in rufous sightings in the East is not any more or less common after an El Niño year, in drought years, in wet, hot, or cold years. It's hard to put a finger on any one common denominator. There is no parental guidance on a migration, but information about migrating has to span the bridge from one generation to the next. Maybe we need to look within, and that means genetic inheritance. But exactly what is passed on? It seems evident that if it were information on the exact winter site, we wouldn't be having all these "stranded" rufous in the Northeast; they'd all be going to a definite place. More likely it is general direction that is carried through generations. With this inherited information neatly tucked away in their little brains, the birds follow a guideline; the rest is experience. If they're successful, whether it's off the beaten path or not, they repeat it and pass it on to their offspring in an ever-widening genetic picture. In other words, birds that accidentally wind up in Louisiana, and then successfully winter there, pass on that information on Louisiana to the next generation. The burgeoning effect may eventually be a population of rufous hummingbirds even hardier than they already are—perhaps an Eastern race. Over the years, the dispersal of rufous hummingbirds to the East may give rise to a subspecies and we may be witnessing this evolution.

The biggest stumbling block for rufous pioneers—at least for now—may be that because their southbound movements occur so early, they settle in at some sites that ultimately are too far north and soon become inhospitable or totally unsuitable. Thus, many of these pioneers perish, casualties of their range expansion effort while those that survive at marginal latitudes create a strong gene pool for future hardiness. It may then be that food supply, not adaptability to weather, will be the limiting factor in new rufous wintering areas. Or future populations may begin the fall migration later and may not stop at Northeast locations at all. It might be suggested that intervention is not the best course of action on behalf of the species as a whole, that without the "weeding out" process of birds not strong enough to make the grade, long-term changes can't occur. Yet one must do what one's conscience will bear. Rather than sacrifice some birds for a possible long-term benefit for others, I follow my heart, giving concern to the individual first.

MY RUFOUS VISITORS

In September 1993, Rosie migrated to my garden. For years I had indulged my imagination with thoughts of a rufous sighting here, but when it really happened I was astonished. Not only did I glimpse this most sought-after visitor to the East, but she stayed—and stayed. Finally, in November, she was brought indoors to spend the winter in my sunroom. Rosie was my introduction to the rufous. Oh, I had seen them before, during their migration through Arizona. I marveled at one particular loud and pugnacious male that claimed everything in a Senoita garden, and I got the impression that the little bully would have fought with himself had there not been anyone else there to push around. But this was different. I got to know Rosie intimately. She charmed me almost instantly with her feisty, endearing personality, and she will always occupy a very special place in my heart. I learned much about the rufous hummingbird as she gave me so very much to observe— her hunting and bathing techniques, her interest in nesting

Rosie—my introduction to the rufous hummingbird

material, the chronology of her molt (except the tail), her behavior toward the rubythroats while she was in my garden, her floral preferences, her personality. When we parted company, I was happy for her and sad for me, but optimistically anticipated seeing her again some day.

When I released Rosie, I remember my husband, himself quite taken by the extraordinary experience, saying to me, "You'll probably never see another rufous." My response was, "Well, you never know."

In December 1994, I had a call from a man regarding an "off course" rufous in Minnesota. No hummingbird—not even our hardy little rufous—could ever make it through a rugged Minnesota winter. An airline company had agreed, as a public service gesture, to transport the bird to a warmer place. The man wanted suggestions about how to capture it. And there were an adult male at Cambridge, New York, and a juvenile in New Bedford, Massachusetts, for the same month. So when I received a call for help in December about a rufous that had taken up residence in an East Hartford, Connecticut, garden, I was not surprised, but I was concerned. The bird had been there since September. And while the weather had thus far not been too severe, the forecast was for a change to a more wintery trend. Again, the worry was not the cold per se, but sustained cold coupled with a lack of available protein and an inability to keep the nectar thawed in the feeders. The constant stream of birdwatchers adding this rufous to their life list had dwindled, but fortunately one of those visitors had given the bird's hostess some protein powder to add to the nectar, so the bird was doing well. Diet seems especially important, and protein may be even more important to these birds than nectar. Nectar gives quick energy, but most of these birds "stranded" in the Northeast aren't really very active—they need to keep warm and nourished. Sugar doesn't cut it. The Cambridge bird was brought here in December, after having lived on a steady diet of sugar-water. He was banded, weighed, and measured—and found to be obese. The bird lived only a few days, weakened, and died. I suppose that's bound to happen eventually—it's inevitable. But I always feel so personally responsible for a bird while it's here. Of course, I think of what I might have done differently. Perhaps that bird should have been weaned off the steady sugar-water diet and gradually introduced to a complete and proper diet. Under similar circumstances in the future, that is the way it will be handled. After examining all factors, the only thing we have been able to attribute his death to is diet. It may be that the bird reached a point where it just could not assimilate any food other than the sugar-water.

Days were getting shorter and colder. There was no way to predict the severity of the winter ahead, but one thing was certain: with the advent of colder weather, the nectar would freeze in the feeder and there wouldn't be anyone available to change it. My advice, based on the vagaries of a New England winter, was to harbor her until spring.

On December 11, I again called Jane, the bird's hostess.

Temperatures overnight would be zero to five above, and the next day would not rise above freezing. It seemed time to act. I got the capture cage ready, made a copy of my federal permit, and told her to call me as soon as she saw the bird the next morning. I was ready to go. Right from the start, this bird was different from Rosie—she was an early riser. I received the call at 6:55 A.M.—the bird had emerged from the cedar tree where it had been roosting and was active at the feeder. I was shocked. Although East Hartford is one hundred miles east of my area and might be a *tad* lighter, it was still dark outside.

When I arrived, Pixie, as the woman called the bird, was visiting the feeder and then immediately retiring to the sunniest spot to sit. It is said that hummers don't recognize individuals, but Pixie certainly knew her hostess. She was absolutely oblivious to Jane, who undoubtedly was an accepted part of the garden. I, on the other hand, was a total stranger invading her territory, an interloper, and she'd let me know just what she thought of the situation— and me. As I set up the cage to capture her, she sailed across the yard and hovered in front of my face, effectively scolding me with her chatter and attempting in her "David and Goliath" way to drive me out. I made an immediate assumption that this was an immature female when I saw four red feathers in the shape of a diamond on an other-wise immaculate-looking throat; indeed, as I was later told, the iridescent red feathers had only burst open within days of my visit. (By her release date in early May, that number had increased to fourteen and other new throat feathers were more or less outlined with buffy.)

Capturing a healthy hummingbird was a brand-new experience for me. I knew nothing about the use of mist nets and wasn't about to try anything that had the potential of harming her. My choice was a capture box. My husband made a soft screened box framed in cedar, with a door on one side. Her feeder was hung at the opposite end from the door. When she went inside to use the feeder, I'd close the door from a distance via the attached string. Sounds easy, right? Well it sounded easy to me, too, but Pixie had other ideas. She was a savvy little rufous who wasn't about to facilitate this capture by being cooperative. She was sharp-eyed and quick, and she could detect even the slightest motion in the string and was quite able to differentiate between movement caused by ordinary breezes and me. I had to be careful and would only try to get the door shut while she was sitting at the feeder, away from the door. But even when I sat hidden inside the house, she kept her eye on that string. After several freezing hours and many futile attempts, I was finally able to close the door when the bird entered the capture box. The way her capture was finally accomplished was quite simple. I threw a piece of camouflage netting over myself and sat next to the box with one hand on the door. She seemed to be completely unaware of my presence in that state and calmly passed just inches from my face as she entered the box. Just as calmly I closed the door behind her. Mission accomplished. She appeared

Pixie had much deeper, richer coloring

Pixie's outer three primaries were old and worn, and longer than the rest

Her undertail coverts were unspotted

The most notable difference was the lack of green on the outer tail feathers

Pixie sported her very own bracelet with her very own number

bright, healthy, and alert but she looked so small—and she didn't like being in that box. I put the cage on the back seat of the car, covered it with a sheet to keep her calm during the ride home, and proceeded on a circuitous route, adding at least thirty miles to the trip, to avoid the stop and go of traffic lights. Once in the sunroom, Pixie immediately left the cage, found her feeder of NektarPlus (she had been using the Perky canopy feeder exclusively, so that is the type that was provided), and settled down on a comfortable spot among some branches that had been placed around the sunroom for her.

The following morning I got my first good look at this beautiful young bird, and was promptly struck by how different from Rosie she appeared when viewed up close. She had much richer coloring, with more and deeper rufous throughout. The rufous coloring extended farther across the lower rump and her back appeared to have a coppery glow. The large amount of rufous at the base of each feather gave the appearance that specks of green floated over a bed of copper. Later, as molting replaced her head and facial feathers, she acquired much more color on her face, as well.

The wings were another source of dissimilarity between Rosie and the new bird. Immediately obvious was the warm brownish tone of her primaries, indicative of old, worn feathers. Indeed, as molting of the primaries occurred, the fresh replacement feathers were glossier, had more of a metallic sheen, and were darker in hue. The

outer three—Primaries 8, 9, and 10—on both sides, however, were never molted and revealed more than just color
differences. With both adult and immature feathers on
each wing, a basis for comparison existed that presented
visible evidence of the disparity between adult and immature wing length measurements. The smooth contour of
the wings was lost as the three remaining old outer feathers were noticeably longer than the rest. The oldest primaries also exhibited a great deal of wear and tear and
abrasion at the tips. And it's no wonder; unlike Rosie, who
never hit anything with her wings, this little one constantly sent small flowers flying via her wing tips while she
hovered and drank. So many differences. Even her soft,
undertail coverts were different from Rosie's—they were
unspotted.

The most notable difference between Pixie and her
predecessor was their tail feathers. There was no green on
Pixie's two outer pairs. Even with all the plumage variation
one might expect, this was not insignificant to me. Because
there wasn't the same green separating the rufous and
black on her outer tail feathers that I had seen on Rosie,
and not realizing just how much plumage variation there
can be in the rufous, I questioned her identity. Could she
be an Allen's hummingbird? It is unlikely but not impossi-
ble. The Allen's makes appearances in the Southeast,
although not with the same frequency as the rufous. She
didn't have those characteristic ribbon-thin outer tail
feathers, but the range of measurements for rufous and

Allen's can be very close and, in fact, overlap in almost all characteristics. Since I had these doubts, it was important to have her measured and banded. There are only a handful of people federally licensed to band hummingbirds in the United States, and I believe licenses aren't generally granted unless an apprenticeship has been served. Licensed bander Bob Yunick is not too far away and he graciously consented to come and do the job.

So, in late April, Bob arrived, scale, calipers, and notebook in hand, and he patiently waited while I got Pixie back into her capture box. Again, it took some time. I removed all the feeders except the one in the box, so she used the flowers instead. It was four months later and she was still uncooperative. Bob performed the task gently with a great deal of finesse, and it was interesting to watch the exacting procedure. The majority of her measurements fell within the range for a rufous and so identification of this bird is no longer in question. When he was finished, Pixie was no worse for the wear, but she now sported a little piece of jewelry—her very own bracelet with her very own number. I was able to observe Pixie over the next couple of weeks until she was released, and was happy to see that she didn't peck at it or pay any attention to it at all. In fact, she may have even been absolutely unaware of its presence.

Pixie was a real education to me. She taught me much about rufous plumage. She looked so different from Rosie that I questioned her identity and the more I questioned, the more I delved. And the more I delved, the more I learned about how variable that plumage can be.

Differences between Rosie and Pixie didn't stop at the physical level. The personalities of these two birds were as different as night and day—as were the conditions of their release. When I released Pixie, she stayed here quite a bit longer than Rosie had. After she left the sunroom, I saw her several times as she checked out everything. I'd lose sight of her and then she'd appear again, sitting on the clothesline, at different flowers, at different feeders. Eventually that same morning I heard a hummer on the north side of the sunroom, and it was Pixie at a feeder. I got that one additional morning from her; after that she was gone.

Pixie's stay here was relatively uneventful, especially compared to Rosie's. Rosie made the most of her situation —she settled in here and became very comfortable with her surroundings and interacted with me in a positive way. Pixie, on the other hand, ignored me. She wasn't afraid of me, but she didn't want to make friends, either. I couldn't get her to eat from the hand-held feeder, no matter how hard I tried. The time of her molt wasn't too different from Rosie's. In December, she molted on the throat and acquired a large throat patch. By mid-January, molting of feathers occurred on her face and head; and by late January, replacement of her primaries had commenced. Unlike Rosie, however, molting of the primaries stopped at No. 7. And, finally, like Rosie before her, no tail feathers were replaced while she was here.

*The molt of her
wing feathers stopped at Primary 7*

When Bob Yunick banded Pixie, he asked about my plans for the following year. I promptly said, "Next year I want a pair," followed by "I want two rufous humming-birds." As usual, I wasn't expecting it to happen, I was reaching for the moon.

I left a feeder up late during the fall of 1995 in case Pixie returned, just as I had unsuccessfully done the year before for Rosie's return. By November I had calls from Colorado, Illinois, and North Dakota regarding stranded rufous hum-mingbirds. Then, in mid-November, I received a call from my publisher, Crown. Apparently the people at Duncraft in Illinois had called them with a message for me from Mary Lou Benedict of Bainbridge, New York (a suburb of

Crystal—a particularly beautiful bird

I identified Crystal as an adult female—Her tail provided some clues.

Binghamton), regarding a stranded hummer. When we spoke, she told me of her concern for a hummingbird that had shown up in her garden about one week earlier. She put a feeder outside for the bird, but the nectar kept freezing so she moved the feeder into her sunroom and kept the door opened so the bird could enter at will to drink. Later she thought it wise to close the door while the bird was inside and then get some help for the bird. My mind began to work. Experience told me that it was probably too late in the year for it to be a rubythroat. I suspected that it might be a rufous, but since the bird was green, she didn't think so. She called the bird Crystal, a name chosen by the grandchildren of her friend. Mary Lou had a small fuchsia plant with some small bare branches embedded in the soil. This is where Crystal liked to sleep, and in fact spent much of her down time on it, as well. I suggested that she put the fuchsia and a feeder in a cage and allow Crystal to go in and out as she saw fit. Then, when Mary Lou was ready to transport Crystal to me, it would be easy to just close the door while the bird slept. We made the arrangements and Crystal, together with her favorite fuchsia, was delivered to me that weekend. She would be spending her winter at this safe haven.

Crystal was a particularly beautiful and healthy-looking bird with rich, deep rufous coloring and clear, sparkling green, a very small throat patch and a beautiful tail with clear, unworn white spots. I identified Crystal as an adult female in her second year—her tail had adult characteris-

tics and her wings had both mature and immature length
feathers. All that told me that in the prior year she went
through an extensive molt except for the outer primaries.
Her feathers were in excellent condition, but the rufous
edges had worn off, so they were not brand-new. While it's
possible that her molt was completed, including the tail,
prior to her arrival, that didn't seem likely, not only
because her feathers didn't appear to be fresh but especially considering what the others had done here.

By the end of the month I received another stranded
rufous call. The report was that an immature female was
hanging around a Stuyvesant, New York, garden and causing concern because of the weather. But the bird disappeared before it could be captured and transported here.

Finally, in mid-December I had a call regarding yet
another immature female, this one in the Little Compton
area of Rhode Island (a state record for the species). She
showed up during the second week in October and her
host, Geoff Dennis, took her in just after Thanksgiving,
when it became apparent that she wasn't planning to
leave. Geoff literally built a greenhouse around this bird
and devised a method to keep sugar-water in the feeders
from freezing. Visits such as these stir up strong feelings
of responsibility within us. Geoff, with that sense and
feeling of responsibility, wasn't entirely comfortable
about having the bird winter there. He called me and we
made arrangements for me to take the bird in. He hadn't
named her, so I suggested "Red." After all, what would be

Some of Red's feathers were emerald, some mint, and some chartreuse

more appropriate for Rhode Island? Geoff agreed, and Red it was.

Red had various degrees of color and iridescence across her back. Some of her feathers were emerald, some were mint-colored, and some chartreuse. Her tail feathers were on the narrow side and one of the middle ones was practically worn down to its shaft.

With the arrival of Red, I would be hosting my fourth rufous in three years. Just a couple of years ago they were accidental in the Northeast, and the first state records for the species began showing up only in the late 1980s. Four rufous, and it nearly was five.

Sunroom Shenanigans

By mid-November, when the call came about the stranded bird in Bainbridge, K-T was on the road to recovery. There were telltale signs of a slight balance problem—occasionally he would have to set his wings into motion to straighten up or a swaying movement might be detected in the feeder as he drank--but all in all, he was doing quite well. The miracle of his progress is a testament to the hummingbird's endurance and remarkable will to survive in the face of adversity. His beak would probably never be perfect, but it would be functional and serve all its intended purposes. I had every reason to expect that a complete recovery would be in order. Of course mid-November was much too late to release K-T, so he would be staying until spring, and time would be beneficial to that complete recovery.

When Mary Lou arrived with Crystal, I could tell immediately that the bird was not a rubythroat but a rufous, an aggressive bird, and that might spell troubles for K-T. What if she were to chase him and he hit his beak again? I transferred Crystal from her cage to the capture box. She would have to stay there overnight until I made adjustments to the sunroom to accommodate a rubythroat with a disability and a pushy rufous. The first thing I did was tack soft screening tautly across the windows. While I have never had a bird hit one of the windows, it might be quite different if one bird were chasing another. With the screening tacked up, a little brightness was sacrificed, but that would be a small price to pay for the assurance that a hummingbird would bounce off screen instead of crashing into glass. The next thing I did was create "private" areas to drink and perch for both birds. A feeder was placed on the north side of the room, behind Crystal's fuchsia and out of sight of K-T. I hoped Crystal would want to continue using the fuchsia perch to which she had become accustomed, and she would follow up by using the feeder closest to it as well—and thus not chase K-T. Having more than one hummingbird would be a new experience for me. I know how mean they can be. I know the rufous's reputation and I didn't want to be responsible for one of them being hurt. The fuchsia, of course, would not really be enough. I could divide the room in half with screening or latticework if need be, but first I'd try natural dividers.

By then, K-T's remarkable little personality had already begun to blossom and he became nosier, more brazen, and certainly more lovable.

Placement of plants was dictated largely by what would best accommodate multiple birds rather than an individual. The honeysuckle would have made a nice natural divider, but that had been placed in such a way that branches hung under the light where K-T liked to sit, so that wouldn't be moved. Instead a large cestrum and the *Pachystachys* were used as dividers between K-T's and Crystal's feeders. I also brought in the "tree" that had been Rosie's and then Pixie's, and which, in between hummingbirds, graces the lath-house. K-T had been using the honeysuckle branches for resting and at times sleeping, but with an extra bird, some additional perching places would be in order.

I released Crystal from the cage, fully expecting her to claim the sunroom as her own. I was sure K-T would be no match for this larger, "aggressive" rufous. Apparently I underestimated K-T's tenacity and ability when it came to defending what he considered his personal territory. He immediately chased her and, surprise of surprises, Crystal didn't defend herself. Instead she retreated to her fuchsia. Apparently that wasn't good enough for K-T—he didn't want to see her at all. I felt sorry for her and tried to divert K-T's attention with a feeder, but he was blind to everything except this new hummingbird in his area. K-T, who had been so silent all along, now began to chatter.

In the beginning K-T chased Crystal to the northeast corner constantly, and eventually she learned to stay there, more or less. Occasionally she'd sit on one of the cestrum or bare tree branches out of K-T's view, but frequently she hid on a crossbrace at the back of the plant shelf. There she could look outside and be out of K-T's view at the same time. To make sure that Crystal got her fair share of food, I brought in another feeder and placed it behind the plant shelf, where only a bird sitting behind the shelf would notice it.

From Day One, Crystal wanted to bathe and went to the waterfall. But that is on the south end of the room and K-T didn't approve, so he would chase her relentlessly before she had a chance to get even one drop on her feathers. Neither would relent, so I then decided to offer some alternative bathing water on the side of the room to which K-T had banished Crystal. A large plastic sweater box, some small flat pieces of bluestone, and a recirculating pump were purchased. I planned to arrange them so water would spill onto flat rocks, drop to a lower level, and continue in that fashion to the bottom of the tray. Then on a trip to a local nursery, I found a lava rock waterfall structure with little plants that was very attractive and seemed appropriate for the hummers, and I bought that. It was already constructed; all I needed to do was add water and plug it in. The only one who ever inspected it, however, was K-T. Crystal still wanted the "big" waterfall.

Red's arrival here wasn't much different from Crystal's. The minute she was released into the sunroom, she was given the "set of rules"—the dos and don'ts of the house. Unfortunately for her, being third in line meant that she would have two bosses—first K-T, who was *everyone's* boss, and the quiet Miss Crystal.

PERSONALITIES

Each bird is different from all others; each has its own personality. K-T was the bossy one and quite the brat, but an underdog. He was also the nosiest and most daring, the most inquisitive, the first to try new flowers, and the one most brazen and curious about me. Crystal was the docile one—usually, the most laid back, the most reserved, and the one most interested in the outdoors. She was also the nicest looking and least active. Red was somewhere in between the other two as far as personality is concerned, certainly the most brazen of the two rufous humming-birds. For the most part, they were too interested in one another to be interested in me—except, that is, for K-T.

K-T was the nosy one, the most curious. He kept himself involved in everything in the sunroom. No matter what was going on, he'd be right there being nosy. There was a pot of nasturtium hanging in a cool, bright spot. The pot had no saucer attached, so when I put too much water in it, some dripped through the bottom drainage holes. To catch the water, there was a plastic container on the floor strategically placed beneath the pot. Since the water would drop about four feet, it made noise—lots of it. Each time I would overwater and K-T heard that noisy drip, he would immediately investigate, going right over to inspect. He approached first from one side, then the other, hiding behind the honeysuckle leaves and watching it from above.

K-T was the first to rebound after a hawk scare, breaking up the quiet with his wings as he bathed or drank. Crystal and Red would not copy; they sat until they heard the outside birds.

Much of my time was spent in the sunroom tending to Peeper, and that gave K-T many opportunities to interact with me. He sat on my hand under the lights, landed on my head more than once, would zip under my lifted arm, rush up to my face and stare into my eyes, touch me with his tongue and stretch when I talked to him. Or he'd fly over to check out my cup and spoon. If only I knew in advance when he'd be doing these cute things. The red sable brush that I preened Peeper with had about one inch of orange coloring at its base. When K-T saw it moving back and forth as I brushed Peeper, he had to come over to investigate. When I'd sit on the loveseat on the north side of the sunroom writing my notes, K-T would come over and sit about eighteen inches above my head just looking at me, watching my every move. His back was to the south side where the other hummers were, but if he heard a squeal or chatter, he'd chime right in—without ever leaving the branch. Occasionally I'd be aware of a hovering shadow or a bit of a breeze as he'd lower himself to check my pad or my pencil, just as a cat tries to play with your pen while you write. As I sat in the sunroom taking notes on their comings and goings holding a pen with a red casing, I became aware of a shadowy figure checking it out. It was nosy K-T, hovering back and forth in front of the pen. He was another hummer that couldn't stay away from my eyes. No matter what I would do in the sunroom, he would immediately float around my head, peering into my eyes. And he enjoyed having me feed him. He didn't like it because it was a treat; I hadn't introduced him to that. He just loved drinking from the hand-held regular feeder. I wonder if he claimed me as part of his territory. I had to be very careful, for I never knew when he would be between my arm and waist, or my body and Peeper's basket—he was always just there. It would be very hard not to love him. He had no reservations about me at all, a possible result of having such close physical contact with me for so long. When I talked to K-T, he would puff up and shift his weight from one side to the other, back and forth, then stretch his wings back and puff up again. It was a little routine that he went through—and all the time he was doing that, he would stare at me.

Many was the time I laughed out loud over K-T's antics. He would look to see my location and then bear down in my direction, deliberately passing as closely as possible to the top of my head. He'd then make a circle, fly back up to the chain, and do it all over again. But first he would wait until I was looking at him. When I bent over and snaked around some plants to change the feeder tucked away under and behind the plant shelf, K-T approached from the other side of the feeder and hovered there, just waiting and looking at me, eye to eye, almost as if he were playing peek-a-boo with me. He surely had a way about him. In fact, whenever I sat down with Peeper, K-T would join us. And as I sat writing notes about this very behavior, someone appeared about two inches from my eyes and hovered there, looking at me. Guess who? K-T, just as though he had been reading my thoughts.

When I walked into the room holding Peeper, just carrying him around to keep him out of trouble, K-T would immediately fly over for a handout. After he finished drinking, he retreated to a twig on the bare tree about eighteen inches from my head. But that wasn't close enough, he had to move to a twig about three inches away and above my face and just look at me. No one could ever tell me that there isn't something special there. And no one could ever keep from falling hook, line, and sinker for this little brat. K-T would hover less than an inch from my glasses and peer into my eyes. What was he looking for? I'd love to know what went on in his mind.

Neither of the rufous were afraid of me—they would do exactly what they wanted to do even when only inches away. They looked at me a lot and I certainly seemed to catch their interest when I talked to them, but neither ever showed any inclination to be as friendly as K-T, Squeak, or Rosie had been, although they watched with great interest when K-T interacted with me.

They may not have been as outgoing toward me as K-T was, but I was trusted and well accepted, and they certainly were curious. For instance, one day as I sat in the sunroom catching up on some correspondence, I was aware of something moving around. When I looked, it was Red, investigating my knee. When we made eye contact, she looked at me for a split second and then slowly moved along. Another time she buzzed around at the top of my head as she tried to figure whether a floral hair tie offered anything she might like. At the very least they were extremely comfortable around me, and I could work two inches away from either one and they'd just sit there, looking.

I wonder what they thought of me. They'd freely chase one another around my head, using it to hide behind, and Red would buzz by, inches away from me as though no one was there. Or when she whizzed by the others—and it was methodical, designed to pass as closely as possible to each one's face—she included me. Was I just another part of the sunroom as were the loveseat, one of the chairs or another hummingbird?

For almost their entire stay here, the girls were dominated by bossy little K-T. Had either rufous been a male, however, things might have been quite a bit different. There's little doubt that a male rufous would have been much bossier than K-T.

One thing that the girls were afraid of was human activity *outside* the sunroom. If they saw anyone out there, they would immediately withdraw to the opposite side of the room, or fly back and forth from south to north and vice versa until the "coast was clear."

One day a large shadow passed overhead—it may have been either a crow or a hawk. There wasn't any avian activity in the garden, but there wasn't any sudden cessation of noise, either. Perhaps they had been quiet for a while and I hadn't noticed as the hummers were active. Crystal had just visited the waterfall. But their awareness of the shadow, even without the accompanying bluejay warning, or sudden quiet, was enough to stop them dead in their tracks. So we know that they take advantage of multiple danger signals.

BUSY MORNINGS—LAZY AFTERNOONS

Each morning before sunrise I'd tiptoe around in the semi-darkness of the sunroom, installing feeders with fresh food in all the favorite spots. I wanted everything to be ready and as they liked it to start their day. There was a basic daily routine that the birds followed: they'd wake up, use feeders, establish daily dominance, visit a few flowers, bathe, and, finally, fly around.

Peeper was the first to wake up almost every morning, and the first thing he would do, of course, was drink. Next, it was Red, and the first thing she would do was visit a feeder to drink. Then it was K-T. The first thing K-T would do is charge Red, then visit some flowers and finally a feeder. Consistently last to waken each morning was Crystal. But once she had wakened and visited a feeder,

After K-T charged Red, he'd visit flowers . . . here it is penstemon

. . . and here it is Salvia elegans

the chattering would begin. All of this within a span of just a few minutes.

Mornings buzzed with activity in the sunroom. Hummingbirds were everywhere—they didn't sit still. While one would repeatedly fly around in a large circle, another would lift six or eight inches from her perch each time the first passed by. Usually Red circled while Crystal lifted, at times making a counterclockwise vertical-oval about twelve inches high. While one was at a feeder, another would be at another feeder and the third would be taking a bath. Then they'd all be flying around. I would hear chips, chatters, squeaks and squeals, and wings, wings, wings all over the place, crisscrossing back and forth in front of one another—just like an airport. Or one might fly up to another, fan its tail in display, and the third would give chase to whichever of the first two had flown off. This was a typical morning scenario, and any of the birds might have been playing any part at any given time. When I would enter the sunroom in the mornings once they were awake, it was more likely than not that I would find K-T hot on the heels of one of the girls. He was such a troublemaker. Birds that had stayed with me in the past were docile by comparison to these. With no competition, they could leisurely stretch, preen, and scratch to their hearts' content. But this year was different and it was lots of fun.

Soon it would be time for a bath. K-T would sit on an elevated perch watching as I sprayed the gardenia leaves. And as soon as I would stop, he descended with feet down and apart, preparing immediately to drop to the water. In fact, if he heard the sprayer when I wetted the tillandsias, he would immediately descend to bathe, whether the gardenia leaves were wet or not. Of all the different places, he liked bathing on the gardenia leaves best. When he would see me at the basket—either bathing Peeper or changing the pad in his basket—he would immediately go to the gardenia to see if its leaves were wet. He would then select one with just the right amount of water and while hovering in front of it, rub his face and chin. He would then select another leaf to slosh around on and, while "doing paddles" to keep himself "leaf-borne," he would accomplish the next part of bathing—rubbing his underparts. Apparently he didn't worry much about bathing his back. He frequently checked the leaves for water with his tongue, one of his favorite ways to explore. When he would cling to one of the leaves to bathe on it, he appeared to be hugging it. But he would stop in an instant to chase a rufous and then immediately return to bathe some more. Afterward he'd retire to a low, horizontal branch on the honeysuckle to dry off. The birds liked that honeysuckle branch.

While K-T was busy bathing on the gardenia, the girls more often than not were vying for the pool at the top of the waterfall. One would sit at its edge—or in the middle of the water—while the other tried to annoy her into leaving. K-T, meanwhile, would continue to slosh around on the gardenia, leaving the plant from time to time to scold the girls—or just stop and hover in midair, looking around

*One would sit on the edge
or in the middle of the pool while the other annoyed her*

K-T would stop bathing to scold the girls

Crystal in the top pool

to see if anyone needed to be sent packing. K-T's bath usually took longest.

The waterfall makes such a nice trickling sound, so tropical or woodsy, and I enjoyed hearing it in the background of their constant chips, chatters, squeaks, and squeals. But every once in a while that trickling sound would come to a halt, making it immediately obvious to me that one of the girls had parked herself in the top pool and pressed herself right up to the stream of down-flowing water. Crystal and Red both bathed that way, facing the hole at the top pool and pushing their bodies right up against it to get soaked. Red even liked sticking her entire beak right into that hole. Neither Rosie nor Pixie had bathed that way, and I had to wonder if one of these girls mimicked the other.

When a freshly bathed Red found a spot to sit and dry off, and the spot was in K-T's line of view, he again stopped bathing to chase her away. As far as K-T was concerned, all the best spots—those under and near the light—were reserved for him and him alone, and should be unoccupied and available at all times. When Red finished bathing and parked herself on a lower branch of the lemon tree to dry off, K-T immediately stopped his bath to chase her away. She was too close, she should dry off elsewhere. Some mornings Crystal would get out of the waterfall and find a spot on the chain to dry off. For no good reason whatsoever, Red would fly over and give her the boot. Not to be outdone, Crystal then found it necessary to travel clear across the room to K-T and give him a little of the treatment she had just received. Usually, however, Crystal and Red would dry off together on the chain, six or eight inches apart, neither feeling in any way uncomfortable about or angered by the other's presence. Within the first fifteen or twenty minutes, everyone had had his or her first bath of the day.

Rosie was the champion bather. She bathed more frequently and in every way imaginable, in and out of the waterfall. Neither Crystal nor Red showed any desire to receive a shower or bathe on a leaf—strictly the waterfall, and only the original waterfall. K-T would occasionally deliberately fly right through the mist while I sprayed the gardenia leaves for him, but that was infrequent and he

really didn't want to experiment with the waterfall or anything else. Now, if I took too long to wet the gardenia, he
would fly to one or the other waterfall, as if examining
whether other water sources had anything to do with his
gardenia leaves becoming wet—but that was lip service
only; he never went in.

Eating, bathing, and a small bit of preening having been
completed, they now had time on their hands. And there
is no better way to pass that time than chasing or otherwise interacting with one another. They'd play a game
similar to musical chairs, although to them I'm sure it was
no game. I wondered how they signal one another and
how they think. They might be sitting quietly, looking out
the window or just doing nothing when, "like a bolt from
the blue," they'd start. K-T and Crystal would face one
another, fan their tails, and chatter. K-T would fan his tail
so wide that the outermost rectrices would be perpendicu-
lar to his body, forming a 90 degree angle on each side.
Crystal would take the perch under the light but K-T
would replace her. Red would then chase Crystal and the
next thing I knew, Red was sitting where K-T had last
been. And in that two or three seconds, they had all
just moved over one spot. Then all would be quiet for a
few minutes, only to start again once they'd moved
around a bit. K-T would be back under the light and
Crystal on a lower branch of the honeysuckle when
they'd both attempt to use the same feeder at the same
time. Chattering, tail-fanning, etc., would ensue, and

First Red sat at the pool's edge . . .

. . . then she entered the water . . .

she frequently stuck her beak in the hole

Crystal and Red dried off on the chain together

appropriately Red, not wanting to be left out, would have to participate in the activity as well. Then all of a sudden, another lull—a quick look around revealed K-T on the honeysuckle branch or under the light, Crystal on the *Aerides* root and Red a few inches from K-T under the light or a few inches from Crystal on a *Russelia* branch— and they'd all be preening. But their uncharacteristic quiet wouldn't fool me for one second. They were just getting ready to raise the devil again. It was neither never-ending nor vicious, and I do believe it was good for them, very good.

When I thought they were getting too rambunctious or too vigorous in their chasing—that is, if Crystal and Red were getting the best of K-T—I would whistle and they would all beat a hasty retreat to a spot where they could sit and decide if there was a danger about. Basically, I felt that Crystal and Red were able to take care of themselves quite well, but K-T was at a disadvantage. I was more inclined to worry about him holding his own, although that had hardly been a problem and K-T had not done badly for himself. Red felt that in order to be dominant, she had to sit wherever K-T was sitting—the branch under the light or the branch of the russelia—exactly the same place on the same stem.

One day Crystal was at the southwest corner of the sun-room, an area where she didn't usually sit. K-T looked all over for her, at the lantana and all the other places where she could usually be found. All the while he looked, he was chirping incessantly, hoping to flush her from hiding. They certainly kept very good tabs on one another.

Identical environmental conditions and opportunity to feed existed for all in the sunroom, but the two species behaved differently in the afternoon. The girls were very quiet in the afternoon while K-T was active. Looking out the window was an afternoon activity—mornings, of course, being reserved for annoying one another. Crystal devoted at least some significant amount of time each afternoon on the diagonal crossbrace of the plant shelf or a branch of the cestrum, just looking out the window. I wondered constantly, "What *does* she look at"? On many afternoons while K-T and Red were engrossed in chasing one another, Crystal would sit on a twig just looking out the window. From time to time her head would jerk quickly to the side as something interesting caught her eye, but for the most part she sat quietly—just looking out. If Red approached and Crystal didn't want her there, I'd hear *tzeept* or *tchu-tchu-tchu*, over and over in rapid succession as Crystal chased her off. What did she look at?

The hummingbirds that have stayed with me in the past have shown little reaction to the weather, each day being more or less just as the one before. These birds were different—on dismal days they were quiet, with each staking out a branch or twig and staying put, for the most part, throughout much of the morning and all of the afternoon. K-T was the least quiet.

For years I've watched hummingbirds retire to the same

spot nightly. That in and of itself is not proof-positive that they *sleep* in the same spot each night, but it's a reasonable assumption. Squeak seemed to give some weight to that assumption as he slept every single night but one at the exact same spot on the same skinny branch. Then along came Rosie. Although she started out sleeping in her "tree," over her six-month stay here she divided her time between the *Aerides* root, cestrum, and shrimp plants. I referred to her as fickle, saying that she was faithful to her habits only while they lasted. But then along came these three to shatter all preconceived notions and expectations of what they would do about sleeping. They made Rosie appear the epitome of habit.

For this winter I was careful not to upset the photoperiod the birds would receive on a traditional wintering ground. I was particularly concerned about Peeper. To be consistent with a normal day length, artificial lighting turned on at 6:20 A.M. and off at 5:20 P.M., thus assuring short days over winter. Days were then allowed to lengthen in the morning and evening naturally with the rising and setting sun. Just before the main light turned off, a small lamp turned on via a second timer and remained on for about one-half hour. This provided a period of dusk for the birds to settle in, if they hadn't already done so. When the main light turned off, Crystal and Red immediately retired to sleeping places, but K-T and Peeper continued to feed. K-T would visit each and every feeder before settling down. By late February, the sun set later than 5:20 P.M. and there was a period of natural dusk in the sunroom rather than the dusk created by the extra light. The birds liked that much better. As soon as the light turned off, the melee would begin—a whir of wings could be heard as they vied for the best sleeping position among their favorite places.

In the beginning K-T moved around frequently at night, owing for the most part to an inability to balance himself properly. He probably felt a bit insecure and would start to flop over, try to right himself, and then move to a different place. So it would not really be fair to compare his sleeping habits to any other. He would start out on the small branch under the light but would invariably move somewhere else—the honeysuckle, the bare branches of Rosie's tree, or usually on a link of one of the chains strung across the sunroom and used to hang plants.

For the first night that Crystal was here, K-T, who had been chasing her all day, felt that she should neither eat nor sleep in his sunroom, yet in spite of the elaborate measures I had taken to provide private places for them, he settled down about six inches away from her on the chain. I could see that K-T slept in a more vertical position than Crystal. I speculated that this was his way of keeping his eye on her. And he stayed put for the whole night!

After that, Crystal pretty much settled on a branch of the lantana at the southeast corner of the sunroom, still less than a foot from K-T, who continued to start out in one place but move to another. Red, who was prohibited by K-T from sleeping near the other two her first night here, found a place for herself on a petiole high up on the *Pachystachys* plant on the opposite side of the room. So for many days, that's how the hummers spent their evenings. By January, K-T stayed put for the entire night.

FAVORITE PLACES—FAVORITE THINGS
THE LANTANA AND OTHER SLEEPING PLACES—The lantana was unique, so it deserves special mention, not because of its flowers, although they are quite attractive to humming-birds, but because it played such a large part in their activity. Each fall I would bring in the lantana and hang it in front of the window while it still had flowers of the past season. But when the last flower faded, the plant would be cut back somewhat severely and placed under the grow light in the basement for new, compact growth and a fresh crop of flowers. The birds had something else in mind. For some reason it became *the* place to be, a favorite spot for quiet afternoons, sleeping, or resting in between attacks.

Early during her stay, Crystal settled on the lantana as her choice sleeping place. Needless to say, once she did, it began to appeal to the others. There's nothing special about the lantana, and in fact, it wasn't even Crystal's first choice of a sleeping place, but everyone wanted it. Each evening Red would try to take the lantana by retiring to it before Crystal got there. One night she even stood firm about taking the spot. When Crystal flew right up to her to "annoy" her, in an attempt to encourage her to leave,

Red stayed anyway and opened her mouth in a threatening gesture to hold Crystal off. But Crystal was tenacious and eventually Red left. Even K-T had to get in on the act, claiming a lantana branch for his own sleeping purposes. It was a little lower on the plant and Crystal basically paid no attention to him. I had to wonder, what do they think they're missing when they don't have exactly what another has?

When Red couldn't claim the lantana as *her* sleeping spot, she settled on one of its branches as her choice resting spot in the afternoon instead. Then each night she would unsuccessfully attempt to claim it from Crystal. So they worked out an arrangement that basically gave Red the lantana in the afternoon until Crystal wanted to get ready to go to sleep. As soon as K-T saw Crystal and Red argue over the lantana, he had to start his shenanigans. Not only did K-T have to sleep on it too, he began to claim it at other times of the day, just to sit, as Red had been doing. K-T took it the next night, too, and on the third night he got there early just so he could claim it first. There are so many other choice places for little hummingbirds in the sunroom, but the grass always looks greener . . .

One day K-T was chasing Red all over the place because they both wanted to sleep on the lantana—an exercise in futility for both of them, I thought, as Crystal wasn't about to give it up anyway—and using me in the argument, chasing one another around and around my head. How wrong I was. K-T got the spot he wanted and

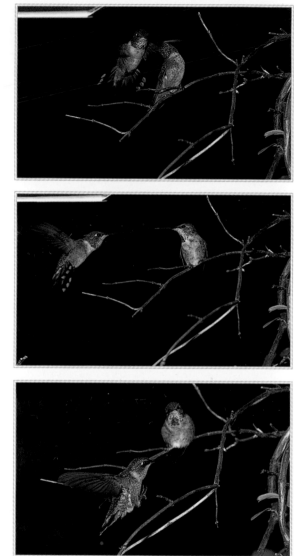

Under the
light . . .

*Crystal
attempts to
annoy Red
away from
lantana . . .*

*. . . but Red
threatens to
hold her off*

*K-T
claimed the
lantana*

Crystal took another. When I think of all the nights Red tried to get that spot but failed I had to laugh at little K-T —such a brat! He never ceased to amaze me. He meant business, he wanted that lantana spot—and he got it.

K-T would sit at Crystal's sleeping spot on the lantana and then almost as though in an act of total defiance, leave, buzz over to Crystal (who was just sitting there bothering no one), stay for a second, and then return to the lantana, almost as if to say, "What are you going to do about it?" At times while he sat there with his tongue sticking out about one-eighth of an inch, he would chirp repeatedly at one of the others, warning her—or them— to stay away.

For the first couple of nights that K-T managed to get a spot on the lantana, he edged Crystal to another spot but shared. Then finally he commandeered it. I'm happy to say that eventually Crystal was permitted to return and remain, but only because even though they were only six inches apart, they faced in opposite directions. By early March and at long last, the three birds slept in the lantana together. Do I need to say that K-T got the best spot (by their standards) while the other two were relegated to inferior positions?

K-T was the one that always remained active longest in the afternoon—probably a species trait—but would settle in first in order to get the best spot on the lantana—as if any one spot is really any better than the next. That same night I watched K-T hide on one of the branches of the passionflower vine—he was waiting to ambush Crystal going to the lantana. I've seen other males exhibit that sort of behavior on numerous occasions and have always marveled at what seems to be an ability to scheme. Certainly if the birds had had a contest to see who was most terrible, K-T would have won hands down.

Eventually Red gave up the lantana for sleeping entirely and moved instead to a horizontal bougainvillea branch. K-T had been successful in driving her away. But once K-T knew that taking the most desirable spot on the lantana was his uncontested right and Red no longer wanted it, K-T lost interest in it and began sleeping on a honeysuckle branch. Crystal stuck it out and stayed with the lantana for a while, but moved back to her favorite branch—the one that had been usurped by K-T. So Crystal wasn't willing to give up the lantana entirely, but did consent to move over, and Red was banished to the bougainvillea and thus the lantana lost its appeal. One night, that little urchin, K-T, showed some interest in Red's bougainvillea but lost interest just as fast when he realized that Red didn't care. Please don't dislike K-T for being such a brat—he was a cute brat and earned every privilege he had, or took. He started out with three strikes against him, one of which is that he is not a rufous, and if someone *had* to be boss, it's best that it was K-T.

In the beginning—when Red was still testing the waters and the other two were still attempting to drive her away, the introduction and adjustment period—she

Sunset over the lantana—K-T (above) got the best spot and Crystal (below) took another

The girls slept only inches from each other on the tree

K-T island-hopped from one tillandsia to the next

They frequently argued over the honeysuckle branch—Crystal and Red

Aloes took precedence over
the feeders . . . K-T with an aloe

. . . Red with an aloe

. . . Crystal visits an aloe

slept wherever she could stay without being harassed. At first it was a petiole of the *Pachystachys*—she was practically driven to it. Later it was the chain—after all, she *wanted* to be near the others. They were less than kind and tried driving her away from that side of the room, so she settled on a large S-hook that holds a feeder. That lasted a couple of weeks—just until she felt that she had been there long enough to assert some authority herself and try for the lantana. But just as quickly as the lantana gained status as *the* place to be, it fell into disfavor and the strangest thing happened: there was a mass exodus to the north side of the room and that became *the* place to be— K-T on a branch of "Crystal's" fuchsia, Crystal on "Red's" petiole, and poor little Red on a bare "tree" branch right near them, but all within two cubic feet of one another. When the leaf, with its petiole, fell from the *Pachystachys*, Crystal lost her chosen sleeping spot. The next night she slept, somewhat awkwardly, on the little stump that remained, but thereafter she chose a place on the "tree" about four inches away from Red, and that's where they slept until their new spring behavior. Why did they (the girls more so than K-T) constantly gravitate toward one another? Once they had adopted that new area and stayed there for more than a week, I seized the opportunity to remove their beloved lantana—they no longer used it anyway—and replaced it with a second, large honeysuckle vine. It had flowers, great places to sit—or sleep— and some juicy little aphids for them to gobble up.

THE SUN AND OTHER WARM PLACES—K-T had pretty much worked out a routine—where he liked to go and what he liked to do—early in his stay. He reveled in warmth and it figured heavily in his daily activities. From the time the light turned on in the morning until the southern sun hit the plants on the west side of the room, he sat under the light and soaked in the heat it emitted. Once the sun entered the room, he followed its path across the sunroom from east to west, until its last rays streamed into the southwest corner. First he sat on a piece of wire on an *Angraecum* orchid. Then he moved westward to a piece of cork bark hosting a tillandsia. From there it was an *Aerides* root midway across the south windows, and finally he moved from one piece of cork bark to the next, island-hopping from one tillandsia to another, accompanying the sun.

Once the girls joined us, K-T had to share the sun. Crystal liked that aerides root and Red liked the russelia branch just behind it, and of course they all liked the lantana at the southeast corner. When the lantana was replaced with a honeysuckle, that became a favorite afternoon perching place and whenever one sat there, another would try to take it away. The south side of the room, but especially the southeast corner, was the area where everyone wanted to be, except on dismal days, when the light's warmth was the hot spot. Another favorite spot—and one that they often argued over—was a spent, horizontal branch low down on the honeysuckle near the light. Why

Tillandsias were the second most popular . . .
Pixie scatters pollen at T. aeranthos

Red visits a tillandsia

it was so appealing, I do not know, except that it provided a clear view of the feeder hanging behind the shelf, as well as the ones on the south —the popular ones. It was the same branch that K-T liked to use to dry off after a bath. It got good sun in the afternoon and a bit of the warmth from the light. How did the honey-

Cestrum elegans *bloomed for the entire length of their stay—Crystal*

Marmalade plant (Streptosolen jamesonii)
flowered for the entire winter—K-T

suckle branch become a favorite spot? In the beginning, when K-T was the only hummer flying around, the branch was never used. Early in Crystal's stay she used it as a sneaky way to approach a feeder or flowers on the south end of the room. Eventually when K-T realized that Crystal used it frequently, it became appealing to him. Once Red arrived and created a place for herself, it became desirable simply because the other two used it.

FAVORITE FLOWERS—The question I am asked most frequently is whether any of my little friends have returned, and the second is about the flowers that I grow for the them. Of course, any discussion of hummingbirds is bound to include or at least touch on their favorite flowers.

With a limited amount of space available for gardening indoors, I'm always on the lookout for new and better plants to grow for my little guests, searching for flowers more attractive to them or hummingbird plants with longer flowering seasons. So the stock would change as I replaced some with other, more desirable offerings. To have just feeders in the sunroom seems far too clinical and not conducive to well-being. Flowers are, therefore, the backbone of the sunroom and are the primary ingredient —in my opinion—in keeping the hummers "happy" and in touch with the outside world. But for the most part, with multiple hummingbirds, they didn't participate as much in the leisurely enjoyment of flowers. The feeders were the most reliable and abundant source of nectar in the sunroom and with competitors to think about, the feeder became the most coveted and protected food source. This behavior was especially noticeable in late winter and early spring. There were some flowers, however, that stood right out for their ability to take precedence over feeders. First and foremost were the aloes, those honey-dripping tubes that hummers find absolutely irresistable. Second were tillandsias. They have consistently been extremely popular. They take up very little space and are very attractive and quite easy to care for. And the hummers love them, inside *or* out.

Now that it appears that I may be hosting hummingbirds every winter, flowers for that period are a big plus. *Cestrum elegans* and marmalade plant (*Streptostolen jamesonii*) have a long flowering period over the entire winter and into spring. Both are very attractive to hummers. The cestrum has proved to be a great winter flowering plant. Blooming began in late fall and continued for the entire time the birds were here, so it provided a constant source of nectar to them, as did tree tobacco (*Nicotiana glauca*)— almost eight months of bloom on a real top hummingbird attractor. Pentas has restrained growth with constant flowers attractive to hummingbirds, and Cape honeysuckle (*Tecomaria capensis*), sporadic for the entire season, is highly desirable.

Some flowers are tried and true and are always very popular with the hummers—*Mimulus cardinalis*, honeysuckle (*Lonicera sempervirens* is the one that I grow and is great under the new lights), tillandsias, *Bouvardia ternifolia*,

Pentas has restrained growth with constant flowers —Pixie

Teco-maria capensis *is highly desirable —K-T*

Always popular is Mimulus cardinalis *—Red*

Bouvardia
ternifolia
—*Crystal*

*Ribes
is a rufous
favorite—*
Pixie

*Crystal
with ribes*

calliandra, penstemon, ribes, arctostaphylos, shrimp plant
(*Beloperone guttata*), and columbine (*Aquilegia* spp.), as well as
members of the acanthus and mint families. Columbine
has continued to a big favorite except that the very beautiful, blue Rocky Mountain columbine (*A. caerulea*) had
much less appeal. This, I believe, is because except when
they are just opening, the flowers are upright rather than
reflexed, and access to the nectar is from above rather than
below. Fuchsias continued to be popular, but less so
indoors than out.

New to the sunroom this year were the citrus trees
(lemon and grapefruit). Citrus, of course, would offer
abundant winter flowers and cover for the birds—
although their use of these two for that purpose was limited—and delightful fragrance for *my* pleasure. Another
new plant that proved very attractive to the birds was
Mimulus lewisii. This plant is a bit more difficult, needing
constant moisture but with good drainage. It was worth
the effort—the flowers are a beautiful rose-colored version
of *Mimulus cardinalis*—and they loved it!

There have been several new plants to grace the sunroom over the last couple of years that have passed the
"hummingbird test." Bolivian sunset (*Gloxinia sylvatica*);
Coromandels (*Asystasia gangetica*); *Clerodendrum splendens;*
blueberry (*Vaccinum* spp.), with bunches and bunches of
manzanita-type flowers (this is not a "house plant" and
must be moved to the garden); *Justicia spicigera;* and
Anisacanthus wrightii, which has been grown here for many

years, primarily for its summer flowers. Now, instead of cutting it back, I've let it grow for some earlier flowers for the winter hummers. Once daylight increased in late winter, buds began to form. This plant may be light sensitive as I've had winter flowers only in years when I had "long" winter days via artificial lighting. Coral fountain plant (*Russelia equisetiformis*) is another favorite with a long flowering season. With the new lights, this sun lover now blooms in winter as well as summer.

I can't say enough about aloes. The hummers loved the spikes of its dense, hanging, tubular flowers, and it was a contest each morning to see who would get to them first during their winter blooming period. They'd hover from one to another, drink nectar, sit on the leaves or spikes, and even revisit flowers that apparently hadn't been drained during the first visit. The aloes were the first flowers to be visited in the morning, frequently even before visits to a feeder, and were probably the most favored of all that had bloomed while the birds were here. When K-T got them first, the girls respectfully left him alone, but when one of the others was first to visit an aloe and K-T decided that he wanted it, he'd chase her away. These flowers are so full of nectar that if they were not drained by one of the birds on a regular basis, the nectar would drip out on its own.

I was very surprised at the hummers' reaction to two orchids. *Dendrobium victoriae-reginae*, a cool grower from Luzon with blue, smallish flowers and a typical nectar-filled

Mints are very popular—K-T

Salvia chiapensis,
another mint—K-T

*The up-facing Rocky Mountain columbine
had less appeal—Red*

Fuchsia continued to be popular—Red

Less popular inside than out—K-T

The beautiful rose-colored Mimulus
lewisii—*Red*

New to the sunroom was Clerodendrum splendens—*Crystal*

spur, was extremely popular with K-T and both girls, and
they visited the flowers very frequently. This was the first
of only a handful of flowers that the birds visited together.
Trichopilia suavis, a very lovely and fragrant species orchid
with a large, beautiful, frilly lip, was the second orchid that
gained favor with the hummers. Crystal paid no attention
to it, but K-T and Red liked it so much they wouldn't stay
away from it. It bloomed while both Rosie and Pixie were
here, but they never even inspected it once. On the other
hand, Red and K-T would even visit these flowers together,
drinking nectar only inches apart—without any arguments.
After the birds were released in spring, the orchid remained
indoors until the weather became much warmer. One day I
took it to the kitchen sink and watered it. When I put it
back on the hook and removed my hand, I found a rufous
primary stuck to my finger—a P.S. from Red.

TINY TYRANTS

While K-T and the Little Angel were confined to side-by-
side baskets, they paid little attention to one another.
Once K-T graduated, however, he became much more
interested in his "brother." But when the girls arrived, he
lost most of that interest and concentrated instead on the
ones that could fly.

   Right from the start K-T felt that the whole sunroom
was his, at least the southern part since he had relinquished the northern half to Crystal. The girls more or less
accepted that, and held their own floating territories—

wherever they happened to be at the time, a perch, a feeder, a flowering plant, the lemon tree, or even bathing water. In other words, K-T protected everything, whereas the girls protected just what they were using. Later that behavior would become evident in another unusual way. And K-T was smart about defending his territory. For instance, he would sit and face away from the girls and listen for the hum of their wings, or fly right around my head, hovering behind me out of sight for a second or two, just waiting for the right time to launch an ambush attack. He'd get so close to me that I could feel the vibration of his wings in my ear.

Eventually K-T accepted their presence on the south side of the room and no longer behaved that way. He saved his energy by only chasing them away from anything *he* liked on that side. In other words, it was okay for them to sit there and use a feeder, but that was all. Once K-T had established dominance in the sunroom, he slacked off a tad but was always boss. After all, he was here first and this was his territory—as was everything in it, including me. We've all come to the conclusion that when K-T collided with that window at the bank, he must have been chasing his own reflection.

The things they did to show how mean and ferocious they can be bordered on the comic. When K-T would feel ornery, he'd approach one thing after another—whether it was one of the girls, the window, or a leaf—with his tail fanned as widely as possible, and hover in front of the

Blueberry has manzanita-type flowers . . . Pixie hangs to reach flowers

object of his aggression. They competed with one another for everything and chased one another constantly—that's an integral part of being a hummingbird. It might start with

Anisacanthus wrightii—*Red*

Aloes were the first flowers to be visited each morning—K-T

one chasing another, but then wind up with the chaser becoming the chased. Most often it seemed to be done for no reason at all except, I suppose, that it's S.O.P. for a

Coral fountain plant (Russelia equisetiformis)—Pixie

They'd sit on the spikes—Red

hummingbird. K-T was the aggressor most often. When a rufous was the aggressor, it was usually against the other rufous. Either way, when the third hummer would see a chase, it would feel the need to participate, except when Crystal was the third bird. She was the most laid back of the three, and she initiated the chase much less often than the other two. And of the three, she was the most likely to sit and watch without participating—or at best, restrict her involvement to vocalization only. Crystal was not without belligerence, she was just the most docile of the three. Whichever of the birds was doing something, that one was at a disadvantage and subject to being chased.

When K-T would see one of the girls feeding at flowers, he'd replace her—just charge in and drink from the flower or feeder as though she weren't there. At times the sunroom was so busy that K-T didn't seem to know whom to watch.

Two feeders on the south side of the sunroom were the favorites and alternated at being the most popular. Every once in a while K-T and Crystal would not let Red use either of them and would even make it difficult for her to use the others. If she approached the feeder closest to the light, Crystal would warn her with a loud *tzeeept*, whereupon Red would turn and leave without using it. K-T would emit a somewhat similar screech to stop her from using the feeder next to the lemon tree. If their warnings weren't effective, a chase would ensue. Once a chase started, the third hummer would invariably join in. No one ever minded his or her own business!

Red, too, had her aggressive moods—quite a few of them, actually—and the longer she was here, the more numerous they became. Occasionally she would chase K-T, but most often it was Crystal. Perhaps the primary concern for a rufous is to dominate a member of its own species or gender. I can't believe that either rufous would accept an inferior status just because K-T was here first and had established the sunroom as his territory. Perhaps it was because K-T was a male and so bossy. Whatever the reason, the girls deferred to K-T more often than not. I found that they were most tolerant of one another when there were more feeders in the room. But, ironically, feeders were just as frequently the source of an argument.

Everyone knows how bossy hummingbirds can be, how one can take over a garden. In fact, they can be and often are downright mean. Does that meanness really relate to food availability? Probably to some degree and at certain times, but it seems that for the hummingbird, being mean is, plainly and simply, just sheer fun.

As we know, K-T "owned" everything. It was comical to watch him keep Crystal away from the waterfall while trying to simultaneously keep Red away from the aloes. He was the most horrible when it came to the other hummingbirds. But likewise, he was the sweetest and most trusting when it came to me—perhaps because I handled him so much in the beginning. He always wanted to be close to or touch me—with his tongue while I worked at the basket, by sticking his beak in the creases between my

K-T replaced Crystal at a tillandsia

finger joints, by hovering in front of me and staring into
my eyes. He constantly interacted with me or used me to
hide behind and attack the others from ambush. K-T

K-T replaced Red at a columbine

When one was in the water, the other would attempt to annoy her

always made me feel that I was a definite part of his world. But how could anything so tiny, so beautiful, and so sweet be so mean?

Nothing special about this vine but everyone wanted it

The rufous hummingbird has the reputation of being the most aggressive of all North American hummers so, when Crystal arrived I was surprised that, irrespective of that reputation, K-T was such a little terror and bossed her around so—or rather, I was surprised that Crystal allowed K-T to get away with it. But I was flabbergasted when Red arrived and K-T continued the barrage of terror, now over both of them. I went through elaborate preparations to assure that each could hide from the others by placing trees in strategic places between feeders, yet all three birds spent more time than not sitting in the same cubic foot of air space with either one or both other birds. Did my little guests like one another after all?

While I never witnessed an act of violent physical aggression, there were plenty of threats and occasionally relentless chases. At times the birds were so loud, chattering and screeching as they chased one another around the sunroom, that I could hear them from my kitchen. Yet I can remember only one occasion when they really were angry. The "argument" was between Crystal and K-T, and it was over the feeder hanging from the back of the plant shelf—the one that had been placed there for Crystal's convenience. Apparently they had both decided to use it at the same time. They fanned their tails and flew here and there in unison, beaks perhaps one-quarter to one-half inch apart, for three or four minutes. After that Crystal sat and emitted one *chip* after another for about five minutes—every once in a while, the string of *chip*s became a chatter. Since Crystal was being so vocal and was sitting about six to eight inches away from the feeder, I presumed she had been victorious this time and was warning K-T to stay away. But when I looked up, K-T was at the feeder. They argued off and on for the rest of that afternoon—Valentine's Day, February 14! That was the one altercation in which Red did not get involved. Perhaps because they were serious, perhaps because Red was the quietest one in the afternoon anyway.

THE GRASS ALWAYS LOOKS GREENER—My little guests seemed to live by the saying, "the grass always looks greener . . ." and if they could have spoken one sentence, I'm sure that sentence would have been, "I want what you have."

There were six feeders in the sunroom for the three active birds, but invariably all three would want to use the same one, whichever one that happened to be at the moment. Likewise, there were three bathing places—counting K-T's gardenia—but both Crystal and Red would want to use the old waterfall—at the same time, of course. And when one was in the water, the other would attempt to annoy her into leaving. When K-T would see me lift Peeper and the feeder out of the basket, he would sail right over for his share. All this because, to a hummingbird, the grass always looks greener.

The desire to have what another uses can run from a favorite feeder to a small branch—for instance, the low, semicircular passionflower vine branch. Nothing special about that branch at all. It offered neither vantage point

Crystal's favorite honeysuckle branch

nor spectacular view of the sunroom or outdoors, yet each took a turn claiming that branch as though to convey superiority to the others. Red had used it in the beginning, but it was usurped by K-T. Eventually, when K-T commandeered another sitting place, Red took it back. Then when Crystal began feeling her oats, she took it away from Red. Each one was constantly tempted and motivated by what the others did or had.

The instant K-T passed Crystal on his way to a feeder, Crystal would emit a *tzeept,* followed by a number of *tchu-tchu-tchu-tchu-tchu* vocalizations. After all, Crystal was sitting on the horizontal honeysuckle branch that they frequently commandeered from one another. But K-T was oblivious and went instead to that dried-up piece of passionflower vine, that naked, curved branch at about mid-height—the place where Red had just been sitting. He took that over instead! Then a few minutes later, he sat on Crystal's favorite honeysuckle branch, as if sitting on these favorite spots obliterated the others' existence. Everything always looks *so* good when someone else is using it because for a hummingbird, the grass always looks greener.

There was no territory per se, it floated with the birds, except that K-T felt that he owned everything. With nothing clearly defined, their attitudes regarding territory may be summed up in one or two sentences. At times, it was, "This is my spot, you go away," or, "I want your spot; go away." They all, however, like the warmth of the light and worked out a nifty arrangement. To start with, the best spot—the horizontal branch under the center—was K-T's. Occasionally Red would take it, but she was usually replaced by K-T. To "replace" her, K-T basically acted as though no one was on the branch and just sat. Crystal took the mostly vertical twig right behind and above K-T, and, when she couldn't have K-T's, Red took the one closest to the light. Crystal was the most skittish of the three, and at times the thumping of her little heart could be seen when she sat under the light with the others.

BIRDS OF A FEATHER . . .

The Yucatán Peninsula to the Louisiana-Mississippi area is one of the major migratory routes taken by a staggering

number of birds passing each spring from the Neotropics
to North America—millions of them, some traveling in
pairs, some in flocks, and some alone, including ruby-
throated hummingbirds. Imagine being on a boat or ship
on a body of water so vast that nothing but the sea is visible for miles around. Then, in the middle of this veritable
"nothingness," a bird as small as a thumb flies out from
nowhere and passes you by. A ship's captain told me of
having seen rubythroats migrate across the Gulf of Mexico
while he was en route from the Yucatán to Texas. One solitary migrant passed the ship, itself moving at about sixteen
knots, in a northeasterly direction from the Yucatán on a
course that would have it arrive at a destination somewhere between Mississippi and western Florida, if the bird
were to continue in its direction. Quite a journey for such
a tiny mite. Since the bird was moving along at a different
rate of speed from the boat, it was difficult to determine
exactly how fast it was traveling, but the captain reported
that it was flying approximately fifty feet above the water.

That picture pretty much typifies the life of the hummingbird. They are notorious loners. Promiscuity is the
rule. They form pairs strictly for the purpose of mating;
incubating, brooding, and raising of chicks are all done
exclusively by the female. Any interaction with other
hummingbirds seems to be of a combative nature. When
nesting season is over and migration begins, the birds—
adult and immature alike—usually go it alone. In the interest of total accuracy, however, I must say that I have

watched many immature rubythroats leave on their migration, and it appears that going it alone is not absolutely etched in stone. Occasionally juveniles migrate together, or at least start out that way—a behavior that appears more common in birds born later in the season. That may also be true for rufous hummingbirds, and may account for two birds appearing together out of the normal range, which has been the case on many occasions. Immediately coming to mind is the pair that appeared at Wave Hill in Riverdale the year that Rosie visited me.

Some birds have such intricate relationships with one another, but hummingbirds, with an energy-demanding lifestyle, are so different. They are solitary little critters, but is that always the case? That lifestyle, while convenient, may not be all that it is cracked up to be for a hummingbird. Maybe they *do* like one another. Maybe they *are* kindred spirits. Keeping more than one bird together for the winter has given me the opportunity to make some observations regarding relationships between them, a somewhat different aspect of their personalities. In spite of the hummingbird's legendary "loneness," my birds gravitated toward one another constantly, particularly Crystal and Red. In the beginning it was obvious that they wanted to sit near one another, but the rule of thumb for amicable communal perching, at least when K-T was involved, was, "we just won't look at one another at the same time." That restriction was dropped as they became more relaxed in one another's presence.

The two girls spent much time together

The three frequently sat in the same cubic foot of air space. More often than not, however, it was two of three, and the two most often to be together were the two rufous hummingbirds. I'm not sure if that was because they are the same gender and/or species, or whether it was just an individual thing. Perhaps they are, after all, kindred spirits. I'd guess that more than 75 percent of their down time— that is, time not at flowers, feeders, or a bath—was spent less than one foot away from the other.

The girls' behavior toward one another—their interaction—made me really stop and wonder. They stayed in the same vicinity as one another, dried off together after their baths, slept within inches of one another, occasionally visited flowers on the same plant at the same time, and frequently just sat around near one another. True, these birds were not living under natural conditions, but certainly the opportunity was there for them to stay away from one another, if they wanted to.

They didn't indulge in customary social behavior such as mutual preening, but they rather seemed to enjoy one another's company. It went beyond just wanting what the other one had. And they kept in touch. If the girls chattered or otherwise "talked" to one another, K-T had to get involved and chatter too—even when he was a distance away and unsure of what was going on.

One event convinced me that while they may be scrappy little sprites in their everyday dealings with one another, there's something between hummingbirds that transcends that feisty, ornery belligerence. Fear can produce the most unlikely of allies or the most unlikely of sleepmates. In late April, during a severe wind and thunderstorm, Crystal and Red proved that. As the storm cell approached, the room grew darker by the second and Crystal moved to the tree and sat there quietly. Within minutes, the rain started, the room became darker still and the wind picked up, causing the branches to sway vigorously on the spruce tree just outside the southeast corner of the sunroom. Red, deciding that it was time to lay low, also moved to the tree. However, instead of settling down on a branch a couple of inches from Crystal, as they had done when they slept there, she sought out the safety and

Crystal and Red sought out the safety
and company of each other during a thunderstorm

company of her "sister," and settled down as close as she was able to get. I doubt whether a piece of paper could have been slipped between them. Crystal didn't object—she was frozen in position, waiting out the storm. That's where they wanted to be. They stayed there, snuggled together like two peas in a pod. When the storm cell passed and the sky brightened, Red left to visit a feeder and it was business as usual again.

And they copied from one another. For instance, there was one lonely flower on the *Kalanchoe uniflora*—the first to open, about two weeks earlier than the others. For the first ten days or so, no one went near it. I even brought it over to K-T in an attempt to rouse his interest, as he was frequently the leader in trying new things. I tried it with the girls as well. No dice; they just weren't interested. Then, one day I noticed K-T draining some nectar—he had finally "discovered" it. Within minutes, Crystal visited the flower and then Red. I watched for the next ten or fifteen minutes as K-T and the girls took turns, like little ants going back and forth, first one then the other, until it apparently was empty. Surely they didn't all "discover" that flower. It's much more likely that they kept an eye on one another and then copied. In fact, each would constantly watch what the others were doing.

On several occasions I witnessed what I consider to be unusual behavior between Crystal and Red. While Red would be sitting, Crystal would fly over and hover just above and away from her with tail fanned in braking position and then touch beaks with her and fly off. She lowered herself slowly and gently to do this; it was not the usual dart and attack. Her action, which reminded me of a feeding action, appeared to be quite deliberate and not aggressive. Red seemed to sense that as well; hers was not a normal defense response, either. I've seen them do it a number of times, but I don't have a clue about what it means.

K-T and Little Peeper went back a long way together, starting out side by side in baskets, but he showed much more interest in Peep before Crystal and Red arrived. Of course, that didn't stop him from being interested in Peeper's feeder. Whenever K-T would see me hand-feeding

Peeper, K-T wanted some too. He would even lower himself almost all the way into the basket to get some.

K-T would come over for a drink from Peeper's feeder and then turn around, holler at everyone else with his chatter, come back, turn around, and scold some more. When I would bring Peep over to drink nectar from the flowers, K-T would immediately sail over to watch, but he never indicated that he wanted to chase him or otherwise behave aggressively toward him. Crystal watched Peeper a lot as well. Whenever I would sit on the loveseat and hold Peeper, I would notice Crystal sitting just a few feet away, watching. I've also seen her looking in the basket for him while I would be holding him out of her view. She was very interested and would watch intently. Red was totally oblivious to him, but Crystal knew there was a hummingbird involved. I don't think she knew just what to make of the situation, but she knew something.

When Peeper would cling to my shirt, Crystal would cock her head and look. While she may have even been slightly apprehensive, nosy K-T would come right over to see what was going on.

K-T frequently circled my head slowly while I sat on the loveseat tending to the Little Angel. Occasionally he would even lower himself to within inches of the bird to get a better look. Somehow, though, no one seemed to consider him a threat and that's probably because he didn't fly around with them.

Crystal was very interested in all that I did with Peeper and watched so intensely when I fed him that I held the feeder with an outstretched arm and offered Crystal some food too. When I stretched my arm in Crystal's direction, K-T got in front of the feeder and turned toward Crystal, chased her, and then came back to use the feeder himself.

K-T would come right over, beak-to-beak, to use the feeder when I was giving some nectar to Peeper. Then he'd hover about two inches away from the hand that was holding Peeper and just look. Often he would come even closer than that and inspect little snags of my cuticles—all the while spying on the bird in my hand. One day he attempted to put his beak in the feeder tube while Peeper was making use of it. Was he jealous?

Hummingbirds may be essentially solitary critters, but even with the constant chasing and occasional mean behavior, I really feel that having more than one made for a healthier, more natural, and—yes, happier—atmosphere, with no boredom.

PLACES TO GO, THINGS TO DO

One of my new and wonderful friends is Miriam Jenkins of Houston. A couple of years back Miriam had a pair of rufous hummingbirds winter in her garden. Sunny, the male, came and went so Miriam didn't see him on a regular basis, but the female, Sparkle, who favored her crape myrtle and loquat tree, was there practically all the time. Sunny migrated northward early in March, a couple of weeks earlier than Sparkle. March 28 was the last Miriam saw of Sparkle. March is the month that I always hear mentioned from other hummingbird fans from the south. It seems to be the preferred month for initiation of migration in birds that winter in the southern states.

Based upon what they've done here, the birds are quite a bit more tolerant of one another in the nonbreeding season and may even seek out one another's presence. But once the breeding season begins, all that changes. I would consider breeding season to begin once hormonal changes start on the wintering ground. And once those changes began, the camaraderie or tolerance that my hummers had exhibited flew out the window. Therefore it was no surprise that a whirlwind of changes, both physical and behavioral, began in March.

A FLURRY OF FEATHERS

There was some feather replacement activity on the throat of all the birds over the winter, but other than the throat, and contrary to what my earlier guests had done, there was a molting drought for the winter season. Once spring rolled around, however, that changed dramatically.

Feathers were everywhere, but it was easy for me to separate and identify the fallen ones. The color of K-T's primaries was a deeper, grayer, brown—a taupe—than that of either rufous, and the rubythroat's outer primaries are somewhat club-shaped and wider at the tip in relation to that of the rufous. Contour feathers for the rubythroat are a deeper green than rufous feathers (which are more to the yellow side of green), and of course, there is never any rufous at the bases or edges of rubythroat contour feathers. Tail feathers would have been the easiest to separate with different color, shape, and pattern for each of the two species.

Separating Crystal's from Red's feathers might be a bit more difficult, but there would be ways to do that, too. Again, the tail would be simple; the shape and pattern were different from each other. For the rest of the feathers, the birds mostly dropped them right where they sat. Additionally, Crystal's coloring was deeper and richer overall than Red's, who looked like a speckled bird with all her shades of green. It would have been a bit difficult but quite possible had Crystal molted at the same time as Red, but since she did not, that challenge never arose.

The only difference in the conditions of captivity for this year's birds, other than the number of birds being kept together, was lighting. When artificial lighting provided "long" days, as it had always done in the past, molting was early, but when winter consisted of "short" days that lengthened naturally with the sun, molting occurred much later and was basically concurrent with and of similar chronology for all three birds.

Word has it that the rubythroat often does not molt its wing feathers in captivity. Squeak hadn't, but his were as perfect the day he left as the day he got here, so it really didn't matter. Crystal's and Red's were in decent condition, so it didn't matter that much for them, either. But K-T's wing feathers had become extremely raggy—wear and tear, I'm sure, from being such an aggressive little bully and chasing the girls around all the time. Feathers can become so worn that a bird may be unable to fly. This was a concern and a factor to be considered with respect to the release of K-T. I wished he would molt those worn wing feathers—in the conventional manner, of course, one pair at a time in succession. Finally, by the end of March, K-T began molting his well-worn primaries. But instead of molting each pair in succession, from the inside out to the leading edge of the wing, as hummingbirds commonly do, K-T lost Primaries 4 through 7 on each side—a whopping eight of his wing feathers gone at one time!* That slowed him down a tad. Then, when those eight primaries were only partially grown in, K-T lost the next succeeding pair.

By early April, Primary 10 was gone, Primary 8 was partly grown in, Primaries 4 to 7 were almost grown in, and his other major primary, No. 9, was so raggy that it was practically useless. But that's not all. The four central tail feathers had come out as well, two of which were just starting to be replaced. I supposed that might impede his braking ability, although in mid-May of this year an extremely plump female arrived in the garden with no tail feathers at all, and she seemed to be totally unaffected by it. With half of his primaries either growing in or missing entirely, K-T's abilities were diminished and he had some difficulty achieving altitude and kept himself less active. Yet he *had* to participate somewhat, so he'd chatter a chorus of *tchews* when the girls chased one another and passed

---

*Primary feathers are numbered 1 to 10, starting at the inside—closest to the body—and working outward to the leading edge of the wing. There are ten tail feathers (rectrices), or five pairs. The pairs are numbered from the center outward, the middle pair being the first and the outermost, the fifth.

over him. K-T was no longer able to maneuver with the same agility and at times had all he could do to elevate himself to a perch. Indeed, on several occasions he had to make a large circle around the room to gradually gain altitude (similar to an airplane versus a helicopter) and I had to keep an eye on him constantly. When he couldn't achieve the speed necessary to elevate himself, he would land on something low and start again. At a time when he would need more protein, K-T became less active and took in less. Because he seemed to be compressing the molt of his flight feathers into a very short period, I thought it best to add the fish food protein to his diet as well.

K-T had started with the others so many times, and turnabout *is* fair play, but since he was at such a disadvantage, I often would stand guard so he could drink in peace.

All winter long K-T kept a snowy white throat. In fact, when I looked up at him while he sat on the chain, he reminded me of a tree swallow, such clean, white underparts and so streamlined from shoulder to tail. By early spring there still were no signs of growing up from K-T. He was a typical male hummingbird bully all right, but there was no "buzzing," as Squeak had done when he began to reach sexual maturity, nor any other masculine behavior or physical characteristics.

With the exception of her tail, Rosie went through a pretty extensive molt, adding to her throat patch and replacing her wing and many contour feathers variously over her body. When Pixie came, she had, within just a few days before her capture, acquired four iridescent red feathers on her throat in the shape of a diamond. By month's end, she had acquired many more red feathers in that area, and through February, molted her wing feathers through and including the seventh primary—and that was it; the outer three were never molted. They were a different color, lighter—evidence of wear, and a different length, evidence of the disparity in wing length measurements between adult and immature birds. At the time I considered that the molt may have been curtailed by being in captivity. But this suspension of or failure to molt the outermost primaries may be a common occurrence not relating in any way to captivity. Three of the four to have stayed here displayed some form of interference in the molt of the wings. Even Crystal, an adult probably in her second year, had both adult and immature primaries when she arrived in November. This appears to be evidence that for her first molt, she *also* stopped at the outer three while in the wild (unless, of course, she had lived in captivity somewhere else).

Somewhere along her way, Red had molted Primaries 1 through 7 before December. Geoff Dennis told me that she had some either missing or in growth while she was in Rhode Island. But when she got here, either feather replacement came to a halt or it had already stopped naturally to be resumed at another time. The molt of her primaries resumed by early spring, and by April 8, Primary 10 was missing—which made her wings appear so very tiny.

Feather replacement—Red

When the molt of the primaries was close to completion, she molted variously and extensively over her body,

One of Red's middle rectrices was worn to a frazzle

including her back and head. So many feathers were replaced that her little gray head looked like a little pincushion with feather sheaths sticking out all around. When she scratched, sheaths scattered and dropped and a powdery white "dust" filled the air around her head and fell like dandruff —we'll call that *angel dust.*

After the feathers of her crown were replaced, the new ones were dull for days afterward. Fresh feathers on Red's rump showed characteristic rufous edgings.

A leopard may not be able to change its spots but can a hummer? Red appeared to change hers almost daily while she was molting on her throat. The pattern of her throat patch appeared to change—one day white was visible where red had been the day before, and vice versa for another day. In one or two places where there had been red, white feathers grew, but the red area expanded elsewhere. One day she seemed to have a solid patch, another day a Fu Manchu type, with white cutting up the center. But in the end, her throat patch changed little from the December explosion to the spring molt. She had only a few masculine type iridescent red feathers on the throat in December, but the number had increased early on and then remained the same until her complete-body, spring molt. Although her iridescent throat patch changed little, she acquired a necklace of bronzy-green spots on the lower throat.

Red would have done quite well with a new tail. One of her middle tail feathers was worn to a frazzle. It showed extreme wear and tear right from the start and by April, little more than the shaft remained. But that was not to be, at least not while she was here.

Crystal molted a little on the throat in December, with no change to her small, existing throat patch. Nothing until her uppertail coverts in March. Once Crystal lost her

The amount of primary growth in a 24-hour period—Red

The amount of primary growth in a 24-hour period—Crystal

uppertail coverts, her middle tail feathers were held slightly parted as she sat—Pixie had also done that and it made her tail appear as though a molt was imminent, but it never started. Crystal commenced an extensive molt late in April, a little later than Red, and very late in the season. When she did start, it was fast and furious with simultaneous head, body, and wing molt—very similar to Red but a bit more compressed.

One thing that I observed when Rosie was here was that she vibrated her tail. It was not something that she had always done—as a matter of fact, it didn't start until after she completed her molt. Since it came right on the heels of her body and wing molt, I remember attributing it to an attempt to dislodge tail feathers and complete the replacement of all her feathers. I have also observed this tail-vibrating behavior in both Crystal and Red. But the odd thing is, all did this in late winter and all started roughly the same time, so for Crystal and Red, it was *prior* to the wing molt. For Crystal, the behavior was often accompanied by sharp, high-pitched vocalizations—*chip-chip-chip*, vibrate, spin around, repeat. This behavior may relate to migration, breeding, or establishing a nesting territory. It has to have some significant meaning, and if anybody out there knows, I wish he or she would tell me.

When I took photos of Red two days in a row, I discovered that her primaries had grown in about one-quarter of the total length in a twenty-four-hour period. I later duplicated that finding when Crystal was molting her primaries.

Photos taken at the same interval revealed a similar rate of replacement for a primary.

Logic tells me that it would be *most* desirable to have the freshest feathers while on territory—after all, for the male, the gorget is likely his most potent symbol of masculinity and is used as a visible badge in his territorial defense or display to a female. It is the last area to molt. For the female, the tail may be her most attractive or potent physical defense attribute. Accordingly, it seems reasonable to expect those feathers to be replaced last; in fact, it is customary for hummingbirds to start tail feather replacement when the wing molt is nearly concluded. But not even one of the females to have spent the winter here has replaced her tail feathers. Even though we're talking about only four birds, that number represents 100 percent, and while four isn't enough to make any generalizations about the molting pattern, it is enough to ask the question: just when does the female rufous molt her tail?

For solitary critters such as hummingbirds, design of the molting process would have to favor continuity of their lifestyle. Carried out, it seems pretty obvious that the molt of K-T's wings could not have been of normal design. K-T also had not acquired any iridescent gorget feathers during the winter, as would be expected from an immature male. He waited instead until spring, long after other molting had begun. As always, I questioned why and wondered if it had anything to do with his accident. Could the damage to his head or the swelling thereafter have affected the glands

The hummers received gifts of fruit flies—K-T and a fruit fly

involved in giving the signals or secreting the hormones
relating to feather replacement? If so, would it—could it—
happen again next spring? I always have so many more
questions than answers and more concerns than solutions.

NEW SPRING BEHAVIOR

ON SAFARI—Insects play a very important role in a
hummingbird's life. While sugars in the nectar they drink
keep their energetic little bodies on the go, the source of
all the substantive properties without which they cannot
live is protein. The hummingbird's primary source of protein is insects.

Conditions in the sunroom were more natural than ever

Crystal was an opportunist, snapping up whiteflies that flew by

before. First, the integrity of the photoperiod had not been compromised and a natural autumnal decrease and spring lengthening of days had occurred. Second, the level of activity came closer than ever before to duplicating what would be found on the traditional wintering ground than when a bird is kept alone over winter. Common sense tells me that active birds will eat more as a result of the extra activity. Of what they eat, the sugars are converted to quick energy, but they are also constantly taking in more protein with each sip that isn't burned off immediately. And so, with their protein needs more than adequately met through the NektarPlus, they were a bit lazy about hunting—or more picky.

The hummers received two gifts during their stay here; ironically, both were quite similar. First, my friends Jim and Brian brought them a large jar of fruit flies that they had started. Then later, Geoff Dennis sent a "grow-your-own" fruit fly kit. Great little gifts to give hummingbirds. But the fruit flies were rarely taken. All three preferred whiteflies and spiders—those were the favorites all winter long. A plus for lantana is that it never seems to be without whiteflies.

Even so, the birds didn't seem to exert much effort to catch anything. K-T seemed to like swarms. He would watch snow as though the flakes were a swarm of gnats and then inch his way around in front of the window, waiting for one to get close enough to grab it. One day I watched him sitting with his mouth open, trying to catch a whitefly as it passed by. But then, almost with a "what the heck" afterthought, he chased it and caught it. After that little hors d'oeuvre, he began moving around among the leaves to flush more of them out. He knew what brushing against the leaves would accomplish; he obviously planned this deliberate action—he wanted a swarm.

Crystal loved whiteflies, and while she would go after something that caught her eye, she was basically an opportunist and was most likely to sit on a branch and wait for something inviting to go by and then snap it up. She enjoyed sitting on that little dried-up lateral honeysuckle branch, and without exerting too much effort, would snatch whiteflies as they flitted around her. I rarely observed Red hunt—in fact, I hardly observed it at all until she began her molt and then she became a very active hunter. K-T was probably the most aggressive hunter and the only one, prior to the molting period, to go on safari, looking for insects. Red took the least amount of insects, making only occasional forays, but that would change.

I remember how active a hunter Rosie had been, patrolling every inch of the sunroom in search of live food. Her insect consumption increased dramatically at the beginning of the year, and I suspected that there might be a physiological need for insects during molt or other premigratory hormonal changes. Now I am firmly convinced that protein is more important to them at certain times during the year than others and that increased insect intake is not the result of a lack of floral nectars during, say, the wet season, but a definite requirement when they undergo certain physical changes.

Once the birds began their molt, their attitude toward protein changed dramatically. Red, who waited to go through a major molt until early spring, also put off her hunting until then. But once her molt began, she suddenly became quite the explorer as she gathered nectar and hunted on safari, just as Rosie had. Quite the little hunter, she was all over—here and there, and everywhere—in search of insects. Blink an eye and she'd be in one place; blink an eye and she'd be somewhere else—on safari. She was obviously driven by an inner need. She had rarely hunted for her entire stay until she started her molt. She would deliberately upset leaves and was very resourceful with her tail. I watched on several occasions as she flicked her lower body at some leaves to upset the whiteflies; that same flick that might be used by someone closing a door with his or her hip. She'd zip over, flick or snap her tail to the side, catch a whitefly, do a little pirouette, zip back, and catch another, flitting in and out, back and forth almost as though she were doing a little dance—dancing with whiteflies from dawn to dusk.

Red would watch as I replaced the lantana after having stirred up and scattered the whiteflies in all directions for her. Then, after seeing what I had been doing with the plant, she decided to help herself. The lower half of her body would move from one side to the other as she moved up inch by inch. Her actions were intentional. She would deliberately brush against leaves to stir up the whiteflies. I remembered how Squeak would wait for me to do that for him at the fuchsia and I marveled at Red's ability—and obvious forethought—to do that very same thing for herself.

Once, while K-T was sitting on the chain right above an area where Red had been hunting, one of his feathers floated down toward the floor, and Red darted over to catch it. K-T just watched.

Crystal didn't go on safari until the very end, but when she did and just as Red had done, she put her heart and soul into it. Ironically, it coincided with the start of her molt.

Once they began to hunt energetically, the girls decided that they liked fruit flies and would even go over to the large opaque jar that held the fruit flies to capture them as they flew in and out. The girls were smart and treated the container as just another feeder as they flew back and forth to visit it each time they wanted some solid food. I had been wondering if I'd ever be able to get rid of all those fruit flies once the season ended, but once Red and Crystal went on safari, that concern was eliminated; anything that moved was fair game and they wiped me out.

PERSONALITY CHANGES—My foremost concern in keeping more than one hummingbird is fighting—one has only to watch them in the garden for ten or fifteen minutes to know how pugnacious they can be. I had to think of something to combat that tendency to meanness that they possess. My theory and method was to supply an overabundance of food and, further, try to keep the feeders as much out of sight of one another as possible. Providing copious amounts of food would mean plenty for the bossiest or most hoggish bird and ample left for the others. In taking clues from nature, birds should defend an area large enough to suit their needs only, anything beyond is a waste of energy. Even though hummingbirds don't always follow that rule, if the birds were to coexist in the sunroom peacefully for half a year, I'd have to provide plenty. Beside the generous amounts of food, a variety of flowers were offered, but it was the NektarPlus that ruled. For the most part, my method worked.

There were six feeders for the three active birds in the sunroom. Each afternoon I replaced all of them with fresh nectar in a second set of feeders. One day I had replaced five and taken the last one down on the south side of the room when the telephone rang. When I went back to finish the job, I noticed K-T, who was molting and not flying that well, chasing both Crystal and Red from one of the feeders on the south. The girls almost seemed to be working in tandem to get at the feeder he was protecting, each making an approach as K-T chased the other. In spite of his reduced flying ability, he managed to hold both of them off. Every once in a while one of them would use one of the three on the north side, but for the most part they were as determined to drink from one particular feeder on the south, as K-T was to keep them away. There was something else I noticed. When the missing feeder was replaced, Red became extremely mean, particularly toward Crystal. I might have just made a mental note of that and let it go except that the very same thing happened a second time—telephone call and same feeder—and then when it was replaced, Red became very mean toward Crystal again. On both occasions, her meanness lasted for the rest of the day and the next day, too.

The springtime change in personality was noticed first in Red. She became vicious toward Crystal, chasing her relentlessly. That mean behavior, while directed primarily at Crystal, was not confined to her totally. Although she wasn't *as* mean to K-T, she chased him as well. True, K-T had been a horrible little bully all winter, but he was never truly mean. Red was.

When Red's personality changed, the camaraderie she had shared with Crystal disappeared and made unlikely allies of K-T and Crystal. Crystal would hide behind the new honeysuckle in the corner to get out of Red's line of sight so I hid a feeder behind some branches and leaves there, in a place where she could sit quietly and drink in peace. The idea was to keep her wings quiet so Red wouldn't hear her. Within hours, however, the other two had discovered the secreted feeder and began using it for themselves, too. Crystal managed to retain it as her territory for a few more days, until K-T decided that if Crystal wanted it that much, it must be good. That honeysuckle quickly became *the* place to sit—and he might just as well use that feeder, too.

Red gave K-T a hard time about bathing, and I had to stand guard, positioning myself between them, so K-T could bathe. When he couldn't get to the gardenia without being harassed by Red, he went to the waterfall and pecked a bit, but could never work up the nerve to plop down right in the stream of water as Crystal and Red had done.

I've often been amazed at the way a hummingbird can fly right on the heels of another, duplicating every twist and turn as though the two were part of a kite string— as if the bird in the rear had prior knowledge of the pattern. While K-T was at his worst and flying with just partial power, the girls—actually, Red most of the time—seized the opportunity to give him a little of his own medicine. I don't know if they were deliberately using his disadvantage against him or were just more aggressive closer to nesting time. At any rate, K-T was slower, with diminished lifting and probably braking abilities. Red could easily have caught him and flown rings around him at any time. Yet when she did chase him, she paced herself to stay just behind him, at a drastically reduced speed, here and there and around and around the room, identical twists, turns and undulations. So obviously it was chasing for its own sake that appealed to Red—she was doing it just for the heck of it!

For a while everyone picked on poor Crystal. Red was being mean all the while she was molting and K-T was, perhaps, taking clues from Red. K-T would go looking for Crystal. He'd hover and then move forward, inch by inch, chattering and trying to flush her out. Once she moved, he would chase her. Then for several days Red was very mean to Crystal—and K-T joined in. They didn't want her to use any of the feeders and chased her constantly to the chain behind the light. Of course, I had to set up additional feeders and try to hide a couple where she could sit and eat in peace, as I had on the honeysuckle branch. As long as they didn't hear her wings, they weren't incited and were less likely to detect her presence. When she finally had enough of their bossiness, she gave it back a bit, but for the most part she was intimidated by them. Red seemed able to detect the unique sound of her own species' wing oscillations or knew the difference between the sound of Crystal's and K-T's wings. And why did Red target Crystal all the time? Perhaps because she was also *the* rival in the sunroom.

Once Red became mean, Crystal no longer wanted to sleep near her—no more communal roosting. She moved back to the south side of the room to the bougainvillea branch where Red once slept. K-T had already broken away and was only loosely part of the group anyway. For a while they slept apart. That coincided with the molt of K-T and Red, insect increase, and normal nesting season. I thought they were following the dictates of nature, but eventually Red followed and they all were back on the south. Just as with their migration to the north, K-T started, to be followed by one girl and then the other. Eventually they split up again. K-T slept on the honey-suckle, Crystal on the bougainvillea, and Red still on the bare tree. Toward the end of their stay here, Red spent much time sitting on low branches of K-T's gardenia—and after having spent much time watching K-T do it, she too began to leaf bathe.

"Sugar and spice and everything nice, that's what little girls are made of"—except when the girls are humming-birds. That bossy stuff was too good to last for K-T, as by mid-March and coinciding with a time of more naturally aggressive behavior, the girls became more feisty, defiant, and belligerent with K-T and would sometimes gang up on him. Red would chase him from a feeder on the south side, and when he got to the other side of the room, Crystal would chase him away from a branch. Even when he'd come over to me to be fed, they'd follow right after him and chase him away from me. I could see changes in the

girls. They became more aggressive—with K-T. I don't
know if it was a result of natural hormonal changes or if
they had just had enough of K-T's bossiness and now realized that they could get away with it. Once they started to
pick on him, he expected me to feed him all the time, but
always wanted to be situated on the side away from
"them." Occasionally he would stop, turn around, fan his
tail, and chatter. Once in a while they'd come over while
he was drinking to call his bluff, but usually they waited
for him to be finished and then chased him.

When Red started her molt, she increased her insect
intake and became very aggressive, particularly toward
Crystal. When Crystal began her molt, she also acquired a
voracious appetite for insects and became equally as
aggressive toward Red, in spite of the fact that she was
generally a more docile bird. Although I hadn't noticed
such behavior with their predecessors, Rosie and Pixie,
they didn't have another hummingbird to be aggressive
toward. For weeks, Red was "feeling her oats." She thought
she was hot stuff, chasing everyone for the sheer pleasure
of it—but I never thought Crystal had it in her.

In late April, Crystal molted those old, juvenile outer
wing feathers. When the molt began, her personality
changed as well. No longer the opportunist, Crystal also
began to go on safari for fruit flies, whiteflies, and spiders
—and she finally began chasing Red around quite a bit.
Crystal was slightly behind Red in both her physical and
behavioral changes. From the time she arrived in Novem-

ber, she allowed herself to be dominated first by K-T and later by Red. But that all turned upside down in late April. What really amazed me about Red's reign as Queen Bully is that she immediately relinquished that position the instant Crystal began to flex a little of her own muscle.

ANOTHER HARROWING EXPERIENCE FOR K-T

K-T's flying abilities had diminished as a result of his compressed molt, and occasionally he had to make a large loop around the sunroom to help generate some lift. At times he didn't make it and would land on a low branch and start again in an attempt to achieve his goal. Under the circumstances, it was incumbent upon me to monitor him frequently, and I did.

One evening I checked when I removed feeders from the room for the night and then, as it was still dusky outside, I checked again a few minutes later just to make sure they were all in a sound sleeping place. But that time there was no K-T. I looked on all the different branches and places where he had slept at other times, but still no K-T. I looked on the floor and at the flowerpot rims. Then I looked at the new waterfall. In the very dim light I noticed something floating in the water at the bottom—as a result of the movement of the water, it was bobbing up and down. It looked as though it might be a leaf but I scooped it out anyway. It was K-T.

I have no idea how he got there. The waterfall was not directly under where he had been roosting when I checked him the first time. It was dusky and he ordinarily would not have moved under such lighting conditions—not voluntarily, anyway. Perhaps he had lost his balance and attempted to lift but couldn't generate the altitude. He was wet, his eyes were closed, and he made no noise when I lifted him—perhaps he had tired trying to free himself. I immediately sucked his beak and nostrils in case any water had gotten in. Then I held him upside down and rubbed him. Finally he cried—a sound we humans rarely hear. I then dried him off and placed him in a basket, at least for overnight. He didn't like that one bit, and I was treated to a barrage of chips and chatters, and his tirade continued on and off for several minutes. No, he didn't like it at all, but he would stay there for the next day, too, while I monitored him. He appeared to be just fine and so I released him back to the sunroom. Everything had happened so quickly the night before that I couldn't remember whether his head was wet or not. All I knew was that K-T had thus far been leading a charmed life. How many times can this bird's life be saved? Soon he'd be on his own and I hoped that he would stay out of trouble.

And what do you suppose K-T wanted to do first when released back to the sunroom? Why take a bath, of course! Obviously his life was not ruled by fear. "Didn't you have enough water the other day?" was all I could say when he inspected his gardenia leaves for bathing water. I knew that I'd breathe a sigh of relief once those feathers were completely grown in. As a precaution—and one which shall remain permanent—I covered the bottom of the waterfall with some screening so no one else would ever fall into the water. And I "bird-proofed" the old waterfall as well by adding rocks to keep the water level up with less volume and then covering the entire bottom with some soft screening. After that, the girls placed a moratorium on its use. Neither would use it the following day—it was different. But the ban only lasted one day.

Regardless of how K-T wound up in that water, I was sure that the bottom line was his wings. He crashed into that glass and couldn't keep his balance; he almost drowned in the waterfall. I didn't want any more problems. So a few days later, I decided to place K-T back in the halfway house until his wings were up to snuff. He didn't like it at first, but he adjusted. The girls were just about ready to leave, but K-T wasn't. I'd keep him there until they left and then he could have the sunroom back and stay for as long afterward as need be.

FROM HUMMINGBIRDS
IN MY HOUSE TO
HUMMINGBIRDS IN MY GARDEN

Wondering when to release the western birds continued to bring me much consternation. The window of opportunity is small for the rufous, as they must be back on territory in time to produce offspring and then return either here or to more southerly wintering grounds before the snow flies again over the Rockies—frequently as early as August. Late March to early April is probably the ideal time to release; that would allow ample time for travel while keeping nesting duties within a traditional time frame. Northeast weather is not cooperative at that time of year, however, and April frequently gives up the most violent weather as arctic and tropical air battle to take control of the country east of the Rockies. The last of winter's cold is frequently well entrenched over the Northeast at that time.

As far as food availability—nectar and insects—is concerned, late April to early May seems to be the most appropriate time for release here in the Hudson Valley. But the best time here may find winter conditions still in existence over the Rockies, where they experience snow, reliably, well into May. The hummers must cross these mountains to get to their breeding areas. That they are a naturally hardier species is without doubt, but one must consider that migrating up the coast early in spring and down the Rockies in late summer is an advantage to the rufous that they can't experience when they winter in the Northeast. Their hardiness, coupled with that milder coastal climate, allows for an earlier spring return to the breeding ground from traditional wintering areas. Since temperatures become more amenable from south to north, birds from Southeast wintering areas probably cross peaks and summits of the Rockies at more southerly latitudes, under more benign conditions. Perhaps they may even make their way through West Coast mountain passes and canyons and then take a "normal" route northward. Whichever way they go, many have successfully returned to the Southeast during subsequent winters, so it is working for them.

There is no such thing around here as a tailwind from the southeast. It seems that whenever breezes come in off the ocean, they invariably carry it with them or wrap around a low pressure system moving up the East Coast and give us the dreaded Nor'easter. In late April there were heavy storms in the East, snow in Wisconsin and Iowa, some snow at the higher elevations of the Rockies—fast-moving systems coming out of Canada and traveling from west to east across the Plains and up into the Northeast, exactly opposite the direction the girls might take. Having the wind at their backs doesn't seem to be possible at these latitudes, but having them fly against the wind can be avoided by releasing them during a calm period. There is no way to assure clear sailing for such an extended voyage over such a long distance, but I wanted them to have at least a two- or three-day forecast of pleasant weather. It simply does not get any easier, but they had places to go and things to do.

RESUMING HUMMINGBIRD LIFE

My, my, how my life has changed. I remember when I'd rejoice at the arrival of spring—the robins, the tulips, even mud as the spring thaw would begin. I'd see signs as early as February—the cardinal's song, lengthening days, crocus breaking through the ground here and there by month's end—when there was no snow cover. But the greening of the earth that had always brought such joy to my heart now means something entirely different. When I see these signs, it reminds me that soon the end of a wonderful winter with my hummingbird friends will arrive. Of course, the end for me means new beginnings for them, with places to go and things to do as they resume hummingbird life.

As our time together drew to a close, I became sadder and sadder at the prospect of never seeing them again. They had brought so much joy—and laughter—to my winter, and I had become so attached. How would I ever bring myself to part with my little K-T? It certainly doesn't get any easier. The sunroom seems to be such a safe haven for hummingbirds during a long, cold winter—an eternal spring with an abundance of everything they need, a hummingbird heaven. But when spring arrives and conditions outdoors change, the sunroom suddenly seems too small for a hummingbird able to travel the entire length of the

Crystal retired to the bougainvillea branch

garden in the wink of an eye. And when what is available outside rivals or surpasses what is offered inside, the time is right.

On their last evening here, the girls made me laugh. It seemed their entire stay could be reduced to two or three minutes of interaction between Crystal and Red. Crystal retired as usual to her bougainvillea branch, but I had to get in there before they went to sleep to get the feeder from behind the honeysuckle. I'd never be able to reach it once she was tucked in—Red was on the *Nicotiana* branch about eight or ten inches away. I disturbed Crystal and she moved to the north side of the room. She returned to the bougainvillea a few minutes later, but while she was gone, Red gave her branch the eye and was just about to land on it when Crystal spied her and sailed over and landed on it first, before Red could take it for herself. No matter how many changes they had gone through, each still wanted what the other had.

That last night was the hardest for me. I watched as they finally settled in on their respective branches, waiting for darkness and sleep. They were so comfortable here. They knew where everything was located and life was easy, the weather great. I felt so sad. *Where will they be this time tomorrow?* I hoped together. I felt that uneasiness in my stomach as they watched me move feeders, and our eyes met.

FIRST, THE GIRLS—I opened one of the east windows to the north of the light. Red was the first to leave. It took her ten to fifteen minutes to realize that there was no longer a barrier there. Once she did, she just left. Crystal took considerably longer; she didn't even look at the window. But finally, she too noticed it and left.

Red flew northeast, but I lost sight of her almost immediately as I was still in the sunroom. Crystal stayed close for about fifteen or twenty minutes, catching insects and sitting here and there, high and low. She didn't try any feeders, but she stopped at a flower here and a flower there. Primarily, however, she was just flying in unbounded freedom, rejoicing. Such a freedom hadn't been available to her in months. It was almost as though she danced with delight as she flitted first from one place then to the next. Although she appeared to be dancing, she was actually hunting—she had developed that insatiable desire for protein since she began her molt, and this represented a new and abundant supply.

Finally Crystal moved to an area of old honeysuckle and lilac branches and approached and charged a hummingbird that had been sitting there—almost as though she were poking or jabbing it—then the two of them flew off. I'm quite sure it was Red, and I hoped they would travel together—that the incident was not just an ordinary hummingbird chase. I didn't see any more of them and by day's end I figured the book was closed on Crystal and Red. *Where were they? How far along had they gotten? Where were they sleeping? Were they together?* I hoped so.

There is no reason why they might not travel together. It is variously and repeatedly reported that hummingbirds migrate alone, even during their maiden migration. While I don't question the accuracy of such reports, I don't feel that this is set in stone, it's not *always* the case. I've seen rubythroats depart together on more than one occasion. I remember one year and one particular young pair that had spent a great deal of time in the garden, constantly chasing one another up and down and around and around the spruce tree trunk. On the morning of September 30, they appeared in the yard as usual, stopping to visit flowers in between chasing one another. Then suddenly they were quite high in the air, flying around one another, intertwining in a figure-eight pattern. They flew higher and higher, gaining an altitude that had not been noticed previously, and then they took off together, high in the sky and straight in a southerly direction. They hadn't been seen to go so far and in such a direction prior to that, and I was surprised at how far aloft they were. They kept going and I watched until they became tiny specks on the horizon. It was an interesting but strangely sad sight; and I've seen other, similar departures. And what about rufous sightings? Why would a pair of "off-course" rufous arrive together a couple of thousand miles out of range, such as the pair that appeared at Wave Hill in Riverdale? They *must* have been flying together.

About 5:45 the next morning, while outside to feed the birds, I approached the viburnum to enjoy its incomparable fragrance. I thought I heard a soft, but distinctive, *t-chip.* "I guess everything will sound like a rufous now," I thought.

Then I noticed a hummingbird at the apple blossom and I heard it again—*t-chip t-chip t-chip*. That *was* a rufous, it is unmistakable. I got closer to get a better look and saw the flash of her tail. It had to be one of the girls, but which one? I got closer still, and she moved to a bleeding heart and then over to a large flowering quince, visited a couple of its flowers, and then sat and watched a rubythroat already flitting around from flower to flower in the shrub. It was Crystal! I couldn't believe it. I hadn't seen her at all the day before after she sailed up to that other hummer and then took off with it. She sat there just looking at me. I wondered if she knew who I was. She wasn't the skittish bird Rosie had been while she was in my garden and allowed me to approach within a few feet. I was so excited and immediately conjured up visions of hybrid hummers —and why not? I've learned that they are so full of surprises—mostly delightful—that nothing should be ruled out. More NektarPlus was made and the door and window opened again in case Crystal wanted to come home. She spent most of the day at the quince, either drinking from its flowers or sitting on its branches.

Crystal surprised me by remaining in the garden after having been released. I had become accustomed to immediate—or almost immediate—departures. I think what surprised me even more is that she didn't take over any feeders. Instead she claimed the flowering quince, perhaps eight feet high with at least an equal spread and thousands of flowers. She'd sit comfortably on one of its myriad branches somewhere at the lower center of the shrub, surrounded by a staggering number of beautiful, apple blossom–colored flowers. This was something she hadn't experienced for a long time. There were flowers in the sunroom, but it was never like this—they were all around her. She shared the bush with scores of bees from large to small, but paid little attention to them except to charge at one every once in a while.

I wondered if she would fatten up and move on in a couple of days—or after the quince finished flowering. I wondered if she'd stay and perhaps claim something else. But most of all, I wondered and hoped that she would nest here.

Orioles like flowering quince too, and they frequently visit the shrub to take nectar, and perhaps pollen. I have watched as many as seven males and two females descend upon the shrub together for a feast. When a beautiful male decided to partake of what was now Crystal's quince, she sailed right over to confront him—the nerve of that bird! She didn't chase him, but I'm sure she wanted him to leave. But the next time the oriole had the nerve to visit the quince flowers, Crystal gave him a piece of her mind, *t-chip t-chip t-chip*, until he departed. After that, Crystal began guarding the quince from a little branch. Similarly, when the fisticuffs of several sparrows' squabbling led them to the quince, Crystal appeared immediately to see what they were doing on "her" territory.

Crystal seemed to be settling in and making herself quite comfortable, and I hoped she would stay. A couple of

Outside, Crystal was surrounded by a staggering number of quince flowers

times a male rubythroat buzzed her—that short, whisking display motion that they commonly make to a potential mate—but she wasn't at all intimidated by it, as the female rubythroats are. She shrugged him off, conveying that "go 'way kid, you bother me" attitude. She couldn't care less about the pendulum display, either—perhaps it's the pitch; maybe it just didn't *sound* right to her.

Finally, a few days after her release, on a lightly rainy morning when nectar production in the quince might not be that copious, Crystal used one of the feeders. And then, before I knew it, she was trying every type of feeder around, even those right near the sunroom, and mastering each one in turn as though she had taken the course, Feeders II—the rufous is such a smart bird.

About midway back on my mother's property line,

which abuts mine to the south, is an old, long, and low outbuilding. On my property, and immediately to the north of the building, are several ten- to twelve-foot lilacs, an immature maple tree perhaps eighteen feet tall, and several densely twiggy bush honeysuckles and several wild raspberry and blackberry bushes—this is the area that Crystal retired to between her lengthy visits to the quince and this is the same area to which Rosie had retired when she was in the garden. It would make an excellent cover area for a nest.

For the first two days after the release of Crystal and Red, while K-T was still confined, I left the door open to the sunroom, but Crystal never showed any interest. But on that first rainy day when the quince was less productive and Crystal had begun using the feeders, she finally approached the door to look in. The screen was then shut as K-T had regained freedom in the room as he became ready to be released. Perhaps Crystal wanted to use the waterfall or chase K-T. Perhaps she saw the familiar NektarPlus feeder or saw some flowers. I wish I had been able to open it so that she might come and go, but I couldn't risk K-T's escaping until I was sure that he was fully able to take care of himself. Soon he would be, and Crystal, of course, would be welcomed—extremely welcomed.

When she couldn't get in, she sat on an old, needleless branch on the spruce and looked around. I called, "Miss Crystal," but she wouldn't even look my way. Then a male

rubythroat instantly appeared and began displaying to her
—back and forth, back and forth. I wonder if her reaction
confused him. She wasn't ready for mating, but she didn't
fly away either. She just looked at him—obviously not
impressed—while he kept it up, displaying from in front
of her, from behind her, from above and below her. Finally,
she darted right up to his face and then took off. I'm sure
Crystal's reaction to his amorous intention was a brand-
new one for him, but that didn't stop him from taking right
off after her. I sat about six feet away, watching this most
unusual picture and kicked myself all the while for not
having my camera with me.

More rain the next day and Crystal was at the sunroom
windows again. While she sat at the large Perky feeder just
outside of the north windows of the sunroom—the same
feeder she had watched so intently from inside—a bluejay
gave a warning call. She instantly spun around and dashed
into the forsythia about twelve to fifteen feet away. I've
seen rubythroats carry on boldly in the face of such dan-
gers on many occasions, but not Crystal. She heeded the
warning just as seriously outside as she had while indoors.
That feeder was her favorite for a while and each time she
used it she'd stop and peer into the sunroom.

Over that night, there was a heavy rain with thunder
and lightning. I remembered how frightened she and Red
had been during a similar thunderstorm and thought about
her all night. I felt very relieved to see her bright and early

the next morning. On sunny days she still spent much time at the quince, but evenings and dismal or rainy days were reserved for the feeders.

I saw her frequently that day, but there was no indication that she was working on building a nest. If she were to stay longer than two weeks, I'd feel hopeful that she would. By the end of the day we had another severe thunderstorm as a cold front passed through. Once it passed and conditions calmed, Crystal made an appearance and drank from the feeders right along with all the others. She certainly fit right in. The next day was markedly colder than it had thus far been, and Crystal moved to the area under the spruce tree, designated it her territory, and "guarded" this spot. That was the most sheltered feeder spot in the garden and it was close to the sunroom door. She spent much time near the feeders among the spruce branches, but occasionally she'd leave to chase a rubythroat.

By Day 7, Crystal had taken over the spruce tree and I was privileged to witness the evolution of her territory. The tree has thousands of twigs and branchlets hidden from view where a highly territorial and enterprising hummingbird can sit unnoticed while guarding her possession. The spruce became Crystal's headquarters. From there she was a one-girl army, chasing all who would *dare* to use any feeder in its vicinity. If another hummer entered her territory, she warned it first with her *tchu-tchu-tchu*. If that wasn't effective, she'd leave her perch and chase the bird.

Usually she would sit somewhere at the lower portion

The spruce became Crystal's headquarters

of the tree, but when there were intruders to chase, she frequently moved to the upper portion. It was all very sneaky on her part. The others entered her web with much trepidation and would then relax when she wasn't seen. That's when she would descend. I believe she was attempting to scare the birds into not coming back. But I didn't want to watch her guard that tree, I wanted to see her bring some nesting material to it and start a nest.

While outside, I watched a male rubythroat sit on the clothesline near the spruce, and deep within its branches I could hear that unmistakeable music to my ears, *chu-tchip chu-tchip tchu-tchu-tchu.* Ignoring her warning, the male left the line and moved to a feeder hanging from a spruce branch. In a nanosecond, he was out and flying off. I wonder why? What part do you suppose Crystal played in that little scenario? Now it was Crystal's turn to be a tyrant. She didn't go out looking for trouble, but heaven help anybody who invaded her space.

I'm not really sure I know what its appeal is, but the spruce tree has consistently been a hot spot for hummingbirds. There are feeders hanging on some of the lower branches, but there are feeders in other out-of-the-way places on my property as well. Yet they all seem to find it irresistible. Immatures chase one another around and around its trunk, spiraling up and down the tree. Each year there is at least one male rubythroat that constantly hides in it or the adjacent lathhouse, just waiting to launch an ambush. One spring, and for a very short time, the returning females held it from the males as a segregated area. And as many others before her had, Crystal found the spruce to her liking. When cold and rain put the kibosh on the quince, Crystal branched out to the feeders and ultimately settled on the ones under the spruce. By and by, the spruce became her territory and she defended it vigorously. She sat here and there, watching all sides. She could easily see out, but the hummers on the outside didn't have even a smidgeon of the advantage she had. The branches close to the trunk are bare and needles are clustered toward the source of light—the outside. She would move from side to side, looking out from behind the needles. From this little fortress, Crystal put the run on anyone who dared to enter the territory she had mapped out for herself.

Over the years I've discovered that the female rubythroats tend to prefer the quiet seclusion of the lathhouse. They like to slip in and have a drink in between nesting duties, without being bothered by amorous or combative males. A Droll Yankee Happy-8 feeder takes center stage in the lathhouse to accommodate them. Until juveniles start to appear in early July, the lathhouse is out of the war zone. There are sunny spots, shady spots, fuchsias and other flowers, and hundreds of places for a hummer to sit and take a break. Crystal expanded her territory and claimed the lathhouse as well as the spruce tree. With this new acquisition, she now had control of four feeders. But I could see her either in the lathhouse or tucked away on an obscure spruce branch, and her behavior mirrored that of the autumn rubythroat lazily sitting around and getting fat, just waiting until that increasing weight reaches a certain point, and that "get going" bell rings. Her ever-burgeoning territory was now extended to include the adjacent lathhouse. Yesterday the spruce tree, today the lathhouse, tomorrow the world! It kept her busy, especially during cold spells when many hummingbirds used the feeders.

There was a tremendous amount of activity in the garden, and right in the middle of it was one tough little gal who managed to keep them all away from her stuff. Crystal had been so docile for most of the winter that I didn't think she had it in her.

A brazen male sailed up and entered Crystal's fortress. *Tzeept* and then he hightailed it out faster than he had gone in. A couple of *chip's* after he left and Crystal settled down

again to await the next intruder. She'd never get a
boyfriend acting that way. If the other hummers drank
from the feeders on the periphery of her "territory," she
wouldn't bother them, so her tyranny was not automati-
cally directed at any hummingbird that she saw, only those
that entered the space she had mapped out for herself.
Unfortunately for Crystal, day after day of cold and/or
rainy weather kept the fifteen to twenty hummingbirds
that were launching their nesting season from this garden
right around the house vying for the feeders or squabbling
just for the heck of it. They kept Crystal busy, especially
the males.

Crystal was extra aggressive toward male hummingbirds. I might be inclined to wonder if this light camaraderie between Crystal and other female hummingbirds
constitutes aberrant behavior, were it not for the fact that
Red seemed to have fit the same mold. Even so, there was
one hummer who was shown quite a bit of tolerance—a
female with no tail feathers. She seemed to react differently toward females in general; she chased them, too, but
was quiet and not nearly as aggressive about it. For some
reason, however, she allowed the "tailless" female to eat
first before she chased her, if she did. Frequently she would
vocalize and not chase her at all. The tail is obviously an
important part of female display, and Crystal may have
considered that bird less of a threat since she had none.
She was so lenient toward that female, allowing her to
enter the lathhouse and use the Happy-8 feeder. Did it

remind her of a fledgling? Did she not see any display mechanism and thus not feel threatened? There are so many of their secrets that I would love to know.

After Crystal would chase another hummer from her territory, she would follow it to the outside of the spruce, just far enough to make her point—as if to say "and stay out." A favorite spot to sit while guarding was on one of the little bare twigs of a large branch that hangs over and practically rests on the top of the lathhouse. From this little hideaway she could see it all in absolute secrecy. It would make a wonderful place for a nest—if only she would. By Day 9, when I watched her at a feeder under the spruce, I could see that she had become quite a little butterball and I didn't have to wait for an answer. She was fattening up and would probably migrate back to her breeding territory. Unfortunately, the longer she stayed, the more difficult it would be to complete nesting chores in time to migrate south under suitable weather conditions. I wished her the best whether she stayed or left, but continued to hope for the former.

That afternoon, Crystal started something new. I was sitting on one of the patio chairs just outside the sunroom. Rajah, my fifteen-year-old Abyssinian, was sleeping on the other, and Crystal was under the spruce, in the lathhouse, and here and there. She seemed to be looking for something. She looked all around the sunroom door and window, on the ground, on low twigs, near the back porch light and back on the ground some more. Then she moved in our direction and stopped just above the sleeping Rajah. She lowered herself until she was about six or seven inches above his head. Could she have been looking for nesting materials? The next morning I put out some cat fur (taken from the cat's brush and not the cat).

Day 11 was the first day in many that was not cold and/or rainy. There was less hummingbird activity in general as they took advantage of a pleasant day to map out available flowers or perhaps start building or refurbishing nests. Crystal spent less time under the spruce and when she was there, she spent much time poking around. I hoped, of course, that she was looking for nesting material.

Crystal continued to be less aggressive toward members of her own gender, and especially lenient toward that female with no tail feathers, but began to spend more time away from the spruce in between feedings. Eventually, long leaves of absence were sprinkled with periodic appearances as she spent considerable time away. I hoped that she might be building a nest, but her ever-widening girth told another story. Deep down I knew it was only a matter of time.

From the time I first discovered that Crystal had remained in the garden, I thought that if she crossed that two-week mark, she might stay and nest. That's exactly how long she stayed. On her fifteenth day here, Crystal was at the spruce bright and early. She sat and looked at me while I changed feeders, totally relaxed in my presence. She then had a long drink and disappeared. A little while later I saw her again but that was the last time. I looked for her all day, but I knew she was gone. That evening, a female rubythroat sat and rested at the spruce between sips. It was final. Crystal was gone.

AND FINALLY, K-T—When Crystal and Red were released, the last of K-T's primaries were coming in, his gorget was almost complete, and he was still molting on the face, crown, and back. Everything was coming together for K-T. He was in the sunroom and progressing quite well, but would have to stay with me a bit longer. It would be best to wait until the molt, at least of his primaries, was finished before releasing him.

When Squeak stayed with me, he showed signs of reaching sexual maturity—he buzzed constantly, "stiffening" the feathers on what should have been his gorget to show them off to their best advantage and utmost brilliance —displaying to, and even mounting, little egg-shaped

Everything was coming together for K-T

flower buds. He even became vicious toward them, stabbing them repeatedly each time he passed. Except that he was a little bully with an impudent personality, K-T never showed any masculine behavioral traits. K-T never gave any indication that he was becoming sexually mature—no buzzing nor displaying to the girls. K-T continued to do very well and his flying abilities seemed to be back to normal. Once he was released back to the sunroom, he showed a great deal of interest in the outdoors, flying to the window and back and forth when another male came to drink from the feeder, but he wasn't chomping at the bit to get out and he still was not displaying.

Then, several days before K-T left, a woman called and told me that her cat had captured a female ruby-throat at her Virginia bluebells. She was able to get the bird away from the cat but it couldn't fly—could I take her? Enter Chloe.

Chloe was a pretty little bird and extremely friendly. Her wings appeared to be perfectly normal, and I suspected that a few days of "R and R" might be all that she would need. It was so early in the season, it is doubtful that any nesting had begun. She started out in a very small screened cage where she could perch and eat. As she began to regain some of her ability, she would graduate to the capture cage and eventually the sunroom. Then she'd be on her way.

K-T was extremely interested in Chloe and his behavior toward her was much different from the behavior exhibited toward Crystal and Red. This wasn't just another hummingbird competitor; this was a female rubythroat and he knew it. All of a sudden K-T began to display—to Chloe in her cage, to tiny tips of broken branches that just hung by a thread, to flowers; to anything and everything. When he wasn't "buzzing" or flying back and forth above her cage, he sat on a branch just above and closest to it, almost as though he were guarding her. K-T was interested and was now more demonstrative to the other rubythroats that visited the feeder at the north window. He lost all interest in me except when I sprayed his gardenia. K-T had grown up! And finally, after so *many* months and so many experiences that other hummers would never know, K-T was ready to be on his own again.

I opened the north window just near that feeder that he had watched so intently. He was free to leave. After fifteen minutes of flying around the sunroom, he finally flew over to the open window. Instead of leaving right away, he inspected the small thumbtack hole in the window's molding from where the screening had been tacked up. Then he went out the open window to inspect the "other side" of the molding and was just about to fly back inside, but stopped as though thinking twice about it . . . "hey, what am I doing?" He turned around, lifted up over the sunroom, and took the usual rubythroat route. My little K-T was gone.

After a couple of hours, a hummingbird sailed right up, looked at me and proceeded to drink quickly from the NektarPlus feeder and then from the flowers of the

Enter Chloe, a pretty and friendly female

K-T was ready to be on his own again

marmalade plant. It was my precious little K-T. In an instant, another male darted over to confront him. K-T turned to chase the other bird, but this was not like Crystal or Red; this hummingbird was serious. For a second or two, they flew back and forth, each trying to gain an advantageous position to be the chaser. Then K-T turned around to leave, but the other bird was hot on his heels and K-T landed in the *Caragana* shrub instead, spun to a face-down position and stayed there—similar to the way a paper plane might just nosedive. *Oh, no,* I thought as I jumped up and ran to see how he was. He wasn't stuck, he was just holding on that way—possibly a deliberately inferior position so the other bird wouldn't hurt him. And as I approached, he left, again with the other bird in hot pursuit. *Will there be no end to the trouble that bird gets himself into?*

A while later, a male was sitting on a catalpa branch with his back to me. I needed to see that face and those pin feather sheaths to know if it was K-T. Then, with the aid of my binoculars, I could see his beak. It was K-T and I was relieved. Still later, I was sitting behind the sunroom on a patio chair, my feet up, when a hummingbird appeared, flew to within three inches of my legs, and hovered there, looking for a feeder in my hand. It was K-T again. He stayed and drank for a minute and then moved over and sat on a honeysuckle branch just a couple of inches from my toes. I saw no more of K-T after that, and I have to assume that he, too, had places to go and things to do.

I think I will miss him most of all. I am constantly asked,

"Which has been your favorite?" My response has always been that I have no favorites—each and every one takes its turn. But K-T *was* special.

As one repeatedly faces the bittersweet inevitability of releasing these birds, it should become a bit easier, but it doesn't. Yet releasing the birds is what makes the whole thing a success. You think about it, plan it, and work up the nerve—but saying goodbye still leaves a lump in the throat. In the beginning I had hummingbirds in my garden all summer, and in the fall I wished they might stay in my house. Now I have them in my house all winter, and when spring comes I wish they might stay in my garden. I suppose everything has come full circle.

One day any one of these birds or one of the others before them will sail into another person's garden to visit some flowers or use a feeder. And that person will stop whatever he or she is doing to admire the beautiful hummingbird for as long as it consents to stay—without ever having a clue about what adventures or secrets that tiny mite has under its wing.

So if you see a little male ruby-throated hummingbird with a slight indentation on the left side of his head just above the eye, a slightly twisted beak, and a tongue that frequently sticks out just a tad, you'll know it's K-T. If you see him, blow him a kiss and let me know.